Her
Father's
Daughter

Other books by Mary E. Loomis

Dancing the Wheel of Psychological Types

Her Father's Daughter

When Women Succeed in a Man's World

Mary E. Loomis

Chiron Publications • Wilmette, Illinois

Library of Congress Catalog Card Number: 94-40574

Printed in the United States of America.
Copyedited by Susan C. Roberts.
Book design by Siobhan Drummond.
Cover design by D. J. Hyde.

Interior artwork was prepared for the author by Graphic Arts, Grosse Pointe Park, Michigan.

Library of Congress Cataloging-in-Publication Data:

Loomis, Mary, 1929–
    Her father's daughter : when women succeed in a man's world / Mary E. Loomis.
        p.   cm.
    Includes bibliographical references and index.
    ISBN 0-933029-88-8 : $14.95
    1. Fathers and daughters. 2. Women—Psychology. I. Title.
HQ755.85.L68   1995
306.874'2–dc20
                                                   94-40574
                                                      CIP

ISBN 0-933029-88-8

Contents

Chapter One

Awakening

The pain was excruciating. It had begun with a dull ache centered in her lower back, but now the ache had intensified. It radiated outward, threatening to block her intention of staying focused. Whether lying in her arbor or standing and dancing toward the tree, nothing changed the intensity of the pain. Nothing she did alleviated the throbbing, pulsing waves. What was this pain all about? She didn't have a back problem. She thought about her life and remembered that the only times she had ever experienced back pain were when she had been eight or nine months pregnant. It wasn't her kidneys. They had told her in the medical tent that, although her kidneys were weak after thirty-six hours of dry fasting, they were working. It would have made some sense if it had been her kidneys. Urinary tract infections were her family's weakness. But, if it wasn't the kidneys, why the pain? What was the pain trying to teach her? There had to be a lesson. Her intent and prayers for this Sundance were to align with the power of the grandmothers. It was with those prayers she had begun her dance to the tree, and now with those prayers she wondered if she could make it through the next day and a half. She didn't know. She would have to take it one hour at a time. She knew there was something here for her to learn, something the grandmothers were trying to teach her through her body. What was it? She continued to dance, moving slowly toward the tree, praying to learn the lesson set before her, praying to align with the grandmothers.

Hour by hour, as she danced or lay in her arbor, there was no relief from the pain. Fearing that somehow her kidneys might be involved, she broke her dry fast in the medical tent with a cup of hot water mixed with lemon, honey, and ginger and took a second cup of the mixture on the morning of the last day. But she would not eat. She was dancing for a vision, and she was determined that, in spite of the pain, she would dance as impeccably as she could.

When the Sundance ended and the coming-together circle was being dismantled prior to the feast, she could hardly move. The tears were still being held back, but barely. "Jerre, Jerre Yarbrough," she thought, "I've got to get to Jerre." She made her way to the area where her friend, a medicine woman who knew the body, had camped. Everything around the tent was packed. It was obvious Jerre was ready to move out. But she was nowhere in sight. Only a young woman, a friend of Jerre's, was present. The older woman struggled to control her voice so that her pain would not be discernible to the young woman.

"Where's Jerre? I need to see her."

The young woman sensed her distress and asked no questions. "I'll get her" was all she said.

Moments later, Jerre, Red Coyote Woman, was there. She was not surprised to see her friend, Mary Ellen, not surprised to see her in pain. Jerre had watched Mary Ellen inside the Sundance arbor, struggling to dance, and she knew her friend had been praying to the grandmothers. Jerre, too, had been wondering what this pain was all about.

"Jerre, I need your help." The words came out slowly, controlled. Mary Ellen was not used to asking for help.

Jerre spread a blanket on the ground and directed her friend to lie down on her back. The woman lay down, grateful to be at last in the hands of a healer. Inwardly, she acknowledged that she had not been able to heal herself; she had not been able to learn the lesson the pain was trying to teach her.

"Breathe into your pain," Jerre instructed her.

Mary Ellen concentrated. She had been breathing into the pain for three days and wanted to laugh at the implication that this instruction was something new, but she couldn't laugh. At this moment, nothing existed outside of the pain. With each exhalation, Jerre, kneeling by Mary Ellen's right side and with her arm under her knees, lifted her friend's knees higher until the knees were touching her chest. The pain was unbearable. No longer could Mary Ellen control her tears or keep silent about her pain.

"I hurt, I hurt." She spoke in a barely audible voice, her head turned to the left and her eyes lowered, ashamed to be seen crying.

"Look at me," Jerre commanded with her soft voice. "Look at me and look me in the eyes."

Tears streamed down Mary Ellen's face as she turned her head as she was bidden.

"Now, tell me that you hurt."

Mary Ellen looked into her friend's eyes and with a muffled voice sobbed, "I hurt, I hurt."

And the pain ceased.

Instantly, a memory/vision of being a young girl, six or seven years old, flooded her mind. She was in the garage of her childhood home arguing with her older sister. They were going out with their parents, and the two girls were quibbling about who was going to sit where in the back seat. Her sister had climbed in first and sat next to the door in what Mary Ellen as a little girl claimed was her seat. Her sister refused to slide over. Mary Ellen had refused to climb across her to the other side. They had reached an impasse. Their father's patience was strained. He stood waiting to close the door for his daughters; his wife, their mother, was already in the passenger seat. With his voice rising in irritation, he ordered her to get in. Her sister, fearing her father's temper, slid across the seat. Mary Ellen took her time. She stepped into the car triumphant, claiming her place, and as she did, she put her hand on the inside edge of the door. Her father's temper was barely under control. He slammed the car door shut, not knowing that he had smashed her fingers between the metal.

Pain flashed up her arm and then her fingers were numb. The little girl did not cry out. As her father climbed into the driver's seat, she spoke.

"Daddy," she began.

"Mary Ellen, I've had enough," her father interrupted. Still the little girl did not cry.

"Daddy, my hand's in the door."

Her father catapulted out of his seat. Her mother, crying, jumped out of hers. Together, they rushed her back into the house, her hand covered with blood, her fingers smashed and throbbing. Still she did not cry. After examining her hand, her parents knew she had to go to the hospital emergency room. And en route to the hospital, her hand wrapped in a towel, her father and mother comforted her, calling her "our little soldier." Now she was more determined than ever that she would not cry. In the emergency room, the decision was made to remove the nail of one finger. Without any anesthetic, the nail was removed. And still she did not cry.

Remembering the scene and the pain that had been stored in her body, the woman knew the lesson the grandmothers were teaching her. It was time to change her myth. No longer did she have to please her father and her mother by being "the brave little soldier." It was all right to cry and it was all right to say she hurt. Pain no longer had to be held in her body, unspoken and unacknowledged.

The woman spoke with Jerre, relating the scene she had remembered and thanking her for helping to release that memory from her body. Mentally, she noted that she owed Jerre a medicine gift. She would take care of that when she got home. Now she needed time to think and reflect. She was exhausted. She thanked her friend again and went off by herself.

As she reflected, she realized it was not just the pain from that particular childhood experience that had been locked away, it was all the physical pain she had felt throughout the years—the bruises that weren't acknowledged until the skin was discolored, the labors of childbirth, the recovery from surgeries. All physical pain had been denied or minimized. Until now, she had never questioned the part of her that had been the little soldier. Through all the years of her life, she had proudly embodied an attitude of brave self-reliance, never questioning where it came from and unaware of how pervasive it was. Well, that was over now, she thought. No longer did she have to deny or ignore any pain she experienced. She also knew it was all right to ask for help; she didn't need to continue doing everything by herself. It was time to change.

Reflecting on her experience led the woman to a deeper awareness and a deeper teaching. True, she had been denying physical pain. But she also had been denying her body. If she began to acknowledge pain, it meant she would also begin acknowledging her body. Her body was capable of registering pleasure as well as pain. She realized that in her stoic denial of pain she had also been limiting her pleasure.

Mary Ellen admitted to herself that she had reveled in being the little soldier because she had wanted her father to be proud of her. She knew her father had loved her deeply and, as a little girl, she had wanted to please him and maintain that loving bond more than anything else in the world. Now she realized she had been living the myth of the little soldier not only in childhood but throughout her life. No more, she thought, no longer. It was time to change that myth, to put away childish things. She would now become a woman, a warrior perhaps, but no longer would she incarnate the myth of the little soldier in her life.

This book is based on the story of that woman who was beset with pain while dancing and praying for a vision during the Deer Tribe's Dreamers' Sundance in the summer of 1989. It is a variation of a story shared by all women who embraced the values of their fathers in childhood and unquestioningly lived in accordance with those values, moving out into society holding their fathers' banners high. This is a story of what it means to be a father's daughter. This is my story. I am Mary Ellen.

Although much has been written about women's journeys and women's stories in the last half of the twentieth century, I feel there has been a void. This work is my attempt to fill that void: to tell the story of women who were imbued with the spirit of their fathers and sought to carry that spirit into the world. These women experienced the positive side of their fathers, and they could be described as having a positive father complex.

The story that I will tell is a woman's story, but it is a story for men, too, because it can help men understand the women in their lives: their mothers, their wives. Most importantly, it will show them how vital a father's spirit is to their daughters.

In telling this story, I am indebted to the women I have known who are father's daughters. I have met them in my consulting room and in professional gatherings. I have found them in literature and classical mythology. I number them among my friends. With very few exceptions, the stories I am telling are those of white women in Western society. Whether the stories can be generalized to women of other races and cultures, I do not know. I do know that the foundation of all these stories is archetypal, transcending race. However, the particular manifestations are shaped by the culture, the society, and the family. And, of course, the stories are also shaped by the personalities of the daughters with their inherent strengths and weaknesses.

Chapter Two

The Many Faces of Her Father's Daughter

What is meant by the phrase *her father's daughter*? Exactly what are we trying to convey when we use those words to describe a woman? After all, since biologically every woman has a father, every woman is technically a father's daughter. However, in Jungian psychology the term does not refer to a biological reality; it is used to denote a particular psychological dynamic, one in which the woman feels her primary parental connection is to her father.

Not all women feel strongly connected to their fathers or to their fathers' world. In fact, some women have a negative feeling about their fathers. For these particular women, the less connection they have to their fathers' values, the better it is, as far as they are concerned.

In this work, the phrase *her father's daughter* is used in the Jungian sense to describe a woman who is imbued with the spirit of her father. This is a woman who, from the time she was an infant, was claimed proudly by her father as his own child. There was never any doubt in the daughter's mind that she was loved. The love the father has for his special daughter, the love he expresses, is typified by Wotan in Wagner's Ring Cycle, as he sings of his daughter Brunnhilde. He describes her as the "happiest pride of my heart," "you whom I love so," and "the laughing delight of my eyes," (Wiedemann 1979, pp. 8–9). This special daughter grew up surrounded by the love of her father, and there was no question in her mind or in the mind of any family member that she was her father's favorite. In psychological terms, a woman who is her father's daughter is a woman with a positive father complex.

With the praise and adoration of the father, a daughter experiences herself as being special and as having a special relationship with her father. The specialness the father recognizes and values in the daughter can be a particular trait or aspect of her personality. Whatever it is, it is something the father can identify with, something onto which he can project his soul. Perhaps it is her intelligence or her athletic ability. It might be her beauty or her strong will. But whatever the trait, the father's daughter is marked because of it as belonging to the father and the father's world.

The daughter probably grew up hearing comments like "You're just like your father" and relishing the comparison, whether it was uttered in praise or leveled in criticism. Or she might have heard something like "Your father would be so proud of you," if she happened to be a daughter whose father was absent, perhaps deceased or overseas serving in the armed forces. In such cases, the bond she developed was often to a spiritual father and not to a human one.

The siblings of a father's daughter, if she had siblings, would have been quick to tell her that she was her father's favorite, and they might have used this fact to their advantage. One woman related how her older brothers would get her to approach their father with requests, believing they had a better chance of getting what they wanted if she did the asking. This woman admitted their assumption was true because the ploy usually worked.

As a young girl, the father's daughter unquestioningly adopts her father's values and glories in being her father's daughter, her father's own. As she grows she is infused with the spirit of her father. For her, "father" is a positive figure. This is what is meant by the term *positive father complex*.

When I began working on this book more than ten years ago, I relied heavily on the Greek myth of Athena to conceptualize the psychological dynamics operating in the women I was labeling father's daughters. Athena, the goddess of wisdom, was born from the head of her father, Zeus. Athena-type women use their intellect, their rational side, in interacting with men and women. Athena is a father's daughter. However, in listening to the many women who shared their stories with me, I quickly learned how limited my initial perception and ideas were. The stories of these women, told in my consulting room, in workshops, and in talks with friends, revealed that it was not accurate for me to define father's daughters, carte blanche, as Athena-type women. Certainly Athena-type women are well represented in the ranks of father's daughters, but there are other father's daughters for whom other myths would be more accurate.

Father's daughters, I found, can assume many different shapes. Indeed, some are like Athena in the way they use their minds to bring civilization and culture to their environments. Others, however, are high-spirited champions of political justice like Brunnhilde, who inspired the warriors to fight and then carried the fallen heroes to Valhalla. Still others are handmaidens of the Lord who serve spiritual ideals, like the Virgin Mary; or athletes who love physical competition, like Artemis; or beautiful women, like Helen of Troy.

Regardless of the many manifestations of the father's daughter, there are certain traits that provide the common ground on which all of them stand. As I examined the lives of the father's daughters I know, certain questions arose: What is it that leads a little girl to emulate her father? Is it a desire to be loved? A desire to belong? I recognized that the answer would probably include affirmative answers to both those questions, but it would include other factors as well. This work is an attempt to explore those questions, to hypothesize possible answers, and to follow where those answers lead.

When a father loves his daughter, viewing her as his special child, a bond develops that is difficult for the daughter to break. Why should she? She is adored, encouraged, loved. But there is a catch. There is a price for this adoration. The love of the father flows freely as long as the daughter is fulfilling the father's expectations. And his expectations are that she will remain a daughter; she will not become his equal, his peer.

The daughter, basking in her father's love and striving to please him, willingly suppresses any part of her personality that does not conform to her father's ideal of how she should be. She learns to be what the father admires. This learning begins when she is a very small child, probably an infant. Unquestioningly fulfilling her father's expectations, molding herself to his ideal, becomes so automatic that she may forget as she grows into womanhood that she is paying for her father's love by denying a part of her own personality.

Father's daughters are secure in their father's love as long as they remain daughters. One of the women who shared her story with me fondly recalled singing and playing the piano with her father. However, when she remembered those times and reflected upon them in her analysis, she realized that she was always the accompanist to her father's performance. She had never been the star or even an equal partner in her duets with him. This woman had starred with others. She had gone into the same profession as her father and had risen to a much higher rank than he had ever attained. Another father's daughter I know was becoming independent, recovering from a painful divorce. For the first time she was doing what she wanted. She purchased a house and was pleased that she had handled the negotiations herself. She was totally unprepared for her father's anger when she informed him of what she had accomplished. He was angry that he had not been consulted or even shown the house before she made the purchase. The experiences of these two women illustrated to me that father's daughters are supposed to remain linked with their fathers in a supportive role. They may be independent with other men or with women, but they are not to become independent of father. And they certainly are not to become his peer.

The particular identity that a father's daughter assumes is determined by several factors. Although her father's values have the most impact, the culture in which the daughter lives and her own personality also influence how she will live her life. The father's daughters I know are a very diverse group. Some are single, others are married, still others are divorced. Some are mothers, others are not. Some are heterosexual, others are lesbian. But despite their differences, there are similarities that unite all these women as father's daughters. The mythic pattern underlying their lives is remarkably consistent. In fact, the dominant themes seem to stay the same across centuries.

Whether told in a fairy tale or enacted in the life of a modern woman, the myth underpinning the life of a father's daughter expresses the following themes:

1. The daughter is secure in her father's love. From the time of her birth, her father makes it obvious that he considers her special, that she is his beloved daughter. Psychologically speaking, she has a positive father complex. The special love her father has for her is noted by her mother and/or her siblings.

2. The daughter, perceiving with the eyes of a child, views her father as wonderful and powerful. Indeed, her father may be the Zeus-like, patriarchal lawgiver, holding wife and children subservient to him. However, it is also possible that in reality he is not powerful at all. He may be an alcoholic, he may be absent, but the home and family revolve around him.

3. The daughter holds the father's values and adheres to them unquestioningly, believing they are her own.

9

4. The daughter lives her life pleasing her father and being affirmed by him in what she does. She struggles to be what he wishes her to be.

5. The daughter is imbued with the spirit of her father and is at ease with men whether she is heterosexual or homosexual. She is spirited, energetic, and competent.

6. Holding her father's values and being at ease in her father's world, the daughter has a vague awareness or belief that women (and the feminine) are not quite equal to men (and the masculine). She may have received this message in subtle ways. For example, her father may have encouraged her with the statement "You can do anything a boy can do," implying that boys can do more than girls. Or the message may have been less subtle, as in the case of a physician father pointing his bright daughter toward a career in nursing but never mentioning the possibility that she might attend medical school and become a physician (and a peer to him).

7. Holding masculine values above feminine values, the daughter elevates the spirit and diminishes the body. Often this entails a denial of fatigue, stress, or physical pain. But in certain instances, it can extend to anorexia or bulimia if the daughter believes her father values thinness and girlishness. Anorexia and bulimia may also result if the daughter believes her father wants her to remain his little, prepubescent girl. The denial of her body can have such an impact on the daughter's enjoyment of her sexuality that she may question her right to be thoroughly orgasmic.

8. Her father usually treats her as an extension of himself, assuming she will want what he wants. Perhaps he teaches her auto mechanics or scuba diving. In some instances, when the mother is absent through death or divorce, the daughter may become a surrogate wife to her father, hostessing his parties, entertaining his friends.

9. There is no history of incest between a father's daughter and her father in the cases I have known. The father may have

10

been a strict disciplinarian and the daughter may have been spanked or punished, but she was never molested.

10. Her masculine energy—that which Jung called a woman's animus—is well integrated and well developed in her outer world as evidenced by her achievements and relationships. However, her masculine energy, her animus, in the service of her inner, private self, is underdeveloped. This paradox will be explored more fully in the following chapters.

The characteristics listed here appear to be traits shared by all women who are father's daughters. These traits typify father's daughters, whether we are discussing Athena, Brunnhilde, Helen of Troy, or Jane Austen's heroines. These characteristics are as true of contemporary women as they are of women in myth and legend.

There is a difference, however, between contemporary women and women in the past. Modern father's daughters are adding a new twist to this ancient theme. They are dreaming and living the archetypal pattern of the father's daughter forward. The old myths and legends end with the daughter separating from the father. Brunnhilde, for example, chooses to burn on Siegfried's funeral pyre and then to ride in spirit to destroy Valhalla and her father. The new myths differ from the old myths in that they reveal the daughter as the redeemer of the father.

Living the myth forward is the evolutionary process of life. If we want to understand today's father's daughters, we cannot discard the old myths and legends. The old stories provide information about the creation and dynamics of the archetypal pattern of a father's daughter. They provide the foundation for what is happening today. And if we look carefully at the symbolic language in those old myths, it is possible that we can learn where the future transformation of the archetype will occur.

The overarching goal of a father's daughter—as she moves on her path toward increased consciousness, living her archetypal myth forward—is identical to the goal of all persons, female or male, as they move to increase their consciousness. The goal for all, although the paths may differ, is to embody the fullness of their unique individuality, to become all they can be. The tasks confronting a particular father's daughter may have elements that apply uniquely to her, but the tasks themselves are similar to those all father's daughters face. Though not everyone faces the same tasks, the techniques that father's daughters employ as they engage the process of individuation can be used by anyone to confront his or her own challenges.

What are the specific tasks of the father's daughter? How is she to move toward actualizing her unique self? To answer these questions, it is often helpful to look at myths and fairy tales and find the symbolic message about the archetypal pattern. An old fairy tale which, I believe, focuses on the psychological dynamics of a father's daughter is "Rumplestiltskin." Perhaps it is a familiar tale, one that was heard often in childhood, one we feel we know well. Now, however, if we listen with our adult ears and process with our adult minds, we may hear a tale we have never heard before.

Chapter Three

"*Rumplestiltskin*"
Her Father's Daughter in Crisis

As children, we were enchanted by fairy-tale fantasies of elves and dwarfs, talking trees and magical beings. Through our imaginations, we were able to enter into a world that, although different from the one in which we lived, was a world in which we belonged. We rode on the wind or the back of a swan and were transported beyond our limiting time-space continuum. When we listened to these fairy tales or read them ourselves, we did not bother to question why we were fascinated by them; the fact was, we just were. Something in those tales touched us, speaking a truth that defied logic. As adults, many of us, concerned with making a living or establishing a family, put fairy tales behind us, turning away from the magical world of childhood, dismissing fairy tales as nothing but playful fantasies. But, as it turns out, there may be more to fairy tales than childhood enchantment.

The Swiss psychologist Carl Jung and his followers discovered that fairy tales reveal truths about human nature. They found that fairy tales, speaking in the symbolic and metaphorical language of the psyche, have within them the bare bones of ancient, archetypal patterns. These archetypal patterns have to do with common spiritual or psychological problems human beings encounter as they live their lives. Jung recognized that fairy tales from different cultures had similar themes. He referred to these basic themes as *mythologems* and took them as evidence for a common ground of human experience. Individuals living in different countries, on different continents, and perhaps even in different centuries could have similar dynamics and experience similar problems. Each fairy tale with its archetypal core, its mythologem, describes at least three things: one, the dynamics of a particular personality structure; two, a problem an individual with that particular personality structure will encounter in her or his life; and three, a solution to that problem.

Fairy tales do not tell us about a specific person in a specific time and place. Rather, they occur within the frame of "Once upon a time" and give only the most general information about the characters. We are told that this is a tale of a king, a miller's daughter, a youngest son, or a wicked stepmother. Individual, distinguishing characteristics that would make the fairy tale specific for a particular person are omitted. Names are rare, and when the characters are named it is because the name is essential to the story. It is Dumling or Cinderella, Sleeping Beauty or the Beast. Fairy tales include only the basic, necessary details of a mythic pattern—a mythic pattern that depicts a psychological problem and its resolution.

The gift of a fairy tale, if we are open to it, (that is, if we will use our adult eyes and ears to reread the story or to listen to it again) is that it will not only reveal in its skeletal structure the components of a particular psychological problem but suggest a solution to that problem.

Although archetypal patterns reside in the core of the human psyche and remain constant through time, they are colored and fleshed out by the unique experiences and personalities of the individuals living them as well as by the culture and time in which the individuals live.

The father's daughter is an archetypal pattern; it is a mythologem. Each woman who is a father's daughter is uniquely incarnating that myth. There is a common ground for father's daughters, as we have seen, yet the archetype of the father's daughter has many faces. A new myth may be emerging for women who are father's daughters, and this new myth will transform the old. Before a contemporary daughter can move to a new myth, perhaps a myth of her choosing, she will need to see the patterns she has been living. Fairy tales offer father's daughters such an opportunity to examine the way they have lived their lives in the past.

When everything is going well, it is a rare person who chooses to change. As the saying goes, "If it's not broken, don't fix it." This is as true for father's daughters as it is for everyone else. But there comes a time when things are not as wonderful as they once were. In the life of a woman who is her father's daughter, something happens that causes her to question her basic assumptions. She may break her bones in an accident and find herself immobilized, unable to care for her children. She may become depressed or suffer panic attacks. She may find herself in a destructive love affair. She may realize that she's an alcoholic.

Whatever it is that happens, she stops and, for the first time, truly reflects on how she is living her life. She sees that she has always striven for perfection and recognizes that she enjoyed the praise from her father and her father's world. Always, she was confident that she was living her life as she was meant to live it. She begins to question the beliefs and assumptions that up until now she had taken for granted.

The father's daughter knows she cannot continue living her life the way she has been living it. Changes have to be made. She knows she is in crisis. But, she wonders, if she does not live her life in the role of a father's daughter, how will she live? The answers are not apparent, but it is possible that ancient wisdom, embedded in a fairy tale, may provide some answers.

The mythological pattern of a father's daughter reaching a point of crisis in her life is told, I believe, in the fairy tale, "Rumplestiltskin." If a father's daughter would look at this tale, she might see a mirror of her inner dynamics, the price she has paid to remain her father's daughter. She might also see what she needs to do so that she can move toward becoming an autonomous human being.

Fairy tales, as I have said, are told in symbolic language. Paying attention to the symbols of the fairy tale is not merely an exercise in amplification, it offers new ways to look at old motifs. In the same way that amplifying the symbols in a dream expands the dreamer's understanding of the dream and its relevance for her life, the amplification of the symbols in a fairy tale expand the fairy tale's message so that it can be understood by many individuals, both men and women. In the case of "Rumplestiltskin," focusing on the symbols of the fairy tale serves a practical purpose for the legions of women who are father's daughters, for the story specifically delineates their tasks as they proceed on their journey toward autonomy.

The tale of "Rumplestiltskin," gathered from several editions of Grimms' fairy tales (Owens 1981, Eliot 1937), begins more or less as follows:

Once upon a time, there lived a father who had a beautiful daughter. Wishing to secure a position for her, he goes to the king and tells him that his daughter can spin straw into gold.

The opening of the tale reveals the dynamics of a father's daughter from the father's point of view. The father has a daughter who is beautiful and special. He believes that she can accomplish great, even miraculous things, and with fatherly pride, he approaches the king and brags about her abilities. Nothing is beyond her, says her father; she can even spin straw into gold. This opening sentence describes what the father expects of the daughter. She is to accomplish great things, and the great things she will accomplish will be in the patriarchal world, for it is to the king that the father travels.

The king symbolizes the dominant force, the hierarchical head, of the patriarchal, masculine culture. The king could be seen as representing the business world, the academic world, the professional world, or even the nuclear family as defined by patriarchal values. Whatever "king" the daughter is presented to, her father expects her to excel. She will be exceptional for, after all, she is his daughter. This is the burden the father's daughter carries: if she is to remain her father's daughter, she must fulfill his expectations. The story continues:

> *The king agrees to see the girl, and when she arrives at the castle, he takes her to a room filled with straw. The daughter is told that she is to spin the straw into gold by the next morning and that if she does not accomplish this task, she will die. The daughter believes she is doomed. When she is alone she weeps, and as she weeps, a little man appears who announces he can spin the straw into gold. What will she give him in return, he asks. The daughter unhesitatingly removes her necklace and offers it to the little man. He sets to work, and by morning all the straw is spun into gold.*

Although it is true that her father has put her in this predicament, the maiden never says, "I can't do this, Dad. It's impossible." Never questioning her father's judgment is typical of a father's daughter. She has enjoyed her father's admiration—in fact, she has thrived on it—and she does not want to disappoint him. In the solitude of her room, the maiden weeps at what appears to be an impossible task.

A modern father's daughter might find herself staying up all night to complete a term paper or finish wallpapering a room. She may be faced with caring for two small children while preparing to be the hostess of an important business dinner for her husband. Whatever the task, she doesn't say, "I can't do it." Alone, she may weep or pray for strength, but never will she say, "It's too much for me to do." What is the cost such a woman pays for being a father's daughter? We are told in the fairy tale that the daughter gives her necklace to the dwarf.

In some versions of "Rumplestiltskin" a neck ribbon is offered as payment to the little man. But whether neck ribbon or necklace, the gift is something that has to do with the throat, that point which connects the heart and the head. Thus, to give up her neck adornment in exchange for completion of the task symbolizes the maiden's sacrifice of her heart-mind connection in order to perform as her father expects her to. In a moment of desperation, believing that she will die if the task is not completed, the daughter severs the connection between her intellect and her emotions.

What the maiden fears is annihilation, that she will cease to exist. But this is a symbolic death. It only feels like annihilation. The real death she fears is the death of her relationship with her father. Psychologically, she cannot envision life other than as she has been living it. In order for her to survive as her father's daughter, living up to her father's expectations, she must suppress her emotions. She sees no other alternative. No longer will she be spontaneous in expressing what she is feeling. Those childhood ways are now past; henceforth, she will control her emotions. It may be that she will deny her emotions completely, claiming to feel nothing. Or she may acknowledge that her feelings matter, and intellectually, she may be able to talk about them. But the connection between the heart and the mind is severed, so that no longer will she be able to stay present in the moment, fully experiencing her emotions. The emotions are too painful. The tale continues:

> *In the morning the king arrives. His astonishment at finding a room filled with gold turns to joy and then is replaced with greed. Wanting more gold, the king takes the maiden to a second room filled with straw and gives her the same ultimatum he gave her the first day: namely, that she will die if all the straw is not spun into gold by the following morning. Again the daughter weeps, again the dwarf comes. This time, when the dwarf asks what she will give him, she offers him her ring. The dwarf takes it and, once again, spins the straw into gold.*

The second transaction between the maiden and the dwarf is more costly for the daughter than the first exchange. The ring, as a circle, symbolizes wholeness; but it is undifferentiated wholeness. The ring the maiden offers as payment symbolizes the potential of her true self. The maiden does not stop to think that the price she is paying for the dwarf's services has escalated. She willingly offers her ring, grateful that once again she will be able to live out her father's expectations. As the fairy tale points out, however, one superhuman feat is not enough to satisfy the king, the dominant figure in the patriarchal world. This king is a greedy king. He wants more and more.

Anyone who has sought fulfillment in a business, a corporation, or a profession knows what it is like to try and placate a greedy king. There is constant competition with others and oneself to stay on top. Work is taken home on weekends after a whole week of long hours. By the same token, a mother who believes she must not consider herself, she must only consider the needs of her children and her husband, knows what it means to strive to feed a greedy king. Father's daughters such as these lose sight of their true being. They end up defining themselves not by who they are but by what they do.

In whatever arena a father's daughter finds herself, the cost of striving to uphold patriarchal values, to feed the greedy king, is nothing less than her potential wholeness. She will remain unconscious of who she truly is.

> *On the second morning, the king sees the room filled with gold and leads the maiden to yet a third room filled with straw. This time he thinks to himself that if the maiden can again spin the straw into gold, he will marry her because, although she is a commoner, no woman in his kingdom would be wealthier. Alone in the room, the maiden does not have time to weep before the dwarf appears. When he asks what she will give him this time in exchange for spinning the straw into gold, the maiden replies that she has nothing left to offer him. The dwarf then proposes she give him the child she will have if she marries the king and she agrees. A third time, the little man spins the straw into gold. In the morning, the king decides to marry the maiden.*

In the third transaction, the maiden bargains away her future. She feels she has nothing to lose. She has no knowledge of the king's intentions and she had never thought of being queen. After all, she has lived her life so far as a father's daughter, not as a queen. The necklace, the ring, and the yet-unconceived child symbolize the increasing cost the maiden pays to live up to her father's expectations and to remain aligned with patriarchal values. With the necklace, she severed her connection with her emotions; with the ring, she chose to remain unconscious; and now, with the promising of her future child, she has given away more than she can imagine.

It is not only father's daughters who make promises with implications beyond what they imagined. I have known priests who took vows of chastity as young teenagers, before they had any awareness of what they were promising. And what of the marriage vows that many people make with the best of intentions, only to discover later that they are living in an impossible situation.

The father's daughter in this fairy tale is a pawn. She is not living her own life. She may have convinced herself, as many women who are father's daughters do, that she is exercising her free will. However, she has not made any free choices; she is doing what is expected of her. Her father's love binds her to him and blinds her to reality. When the king marries her, she exchanges one patriarch for another. The king does not marry her out of love, he marries her because she is wealthy and he wants to own and control her wealth. Her wealth means her resources—her talents, her abilities, her mind. The king wants her as a support, not as an equal.

The maiden in this story creates gold out of straw—gold and not silver. Symbolically, gold is connected with the sun and the masculine element; silver is connected with the feminine. With her abilities and talents, the father's daughter unquestioningly contributes to the wealth of the patriarchy. This could be the contemporary woman who is honored for her contributions to the PTA, the state bar association, or the local church. She is honored to the extent that she enriches the king. In the fairy tale, the maiden becomes the queen. Thus she receives the highest honor the patriarchy—the king—can bestow.

> *After a year or so, a child is born. As queen, the maiden forgets the bargain she struck with the dwarf. The dwarf, however, does not forget, and one night he returns to claim the child who was promised to him. The queen is grief-stricken. She weeps and mourns. The dwarf takes pity on her and tells her that if she can discover his name within three days, he will cancel their bargain and the baby will be hers.*

We are not told the sex of the child, but it does not matter; all children symbolize new life, new beginnings. For the maiden, now queen, new life has begun. She has found a place for herself in the patriarchal realm; she has risen as far as possible for a woman. She has become queen. She has prominence and dominion over many things, but with the appearance of the dwarf and his demand for payment, she now realizes the price she has paid for her success. She does not have dominion over herself. For the first time, she realizes the price she has paid to remain her father's daughter. The queen's grief at this realization is not the same as the tears she had shed out of fear when she was faced with the impossible task of spinning straw into gold. This grief, this mourning, these tears are not for a loss of her life but for a loss of her soul. By fully experiencing the loss and not denying what she is feeling, the queen reconnects with her emotions.

It is at this moment that the dwarf who appears so demanding and sly relents. Seeing the queen's mourning, her authentic, heartfelt grief, the dwarf offers a new option. There is a way for the queen to maintain her connection with her child, to not suffer the loss of her soul, but it will require that the queen change, that she use her wits and her abilities for herself.

Inevitably, for anyone feeding a greedy king, there comes a moment of realization, a moment when the true cost of feeding the king becomes apparent. It is a time of painful recognition, a time when one acknowledges the lack of reciprocity in one's relationship with the king. It is a moment of stunning, sobering intensity when one sees reality as it truly exists, admitting for the first time that the only value one has for the king lies in what one gives to him.

I have known women, and men, who believed that they were valued by the corporate organization in which they worked. Holding that belief, they would work long hours. Twelve-hour days or seventy-hour weeks were not uncommon. Their entire lives were invested in their work. One day, something happened that caused them to reflect. Maybe they were passed over for a promotion and, with shock, watched as someone with less experience and less ability moved ahead of them. Perhaps the person receiving the promotion fit the corporate image more closely than they. Or maybe they were told, "It's just a matter of finances; don't take it personally," as they were dismissed from their job. These are individuals who were feeding a greedy king. What happened to shock them into awareness is what happens to the maiden in the fairy tale when the dwarf demands the child. The dwarf has forced the queen to acknowledge that she has paid with her soul to maintain her role as her father's daughter. She has garnered wealth in the material world, but she is caught in an illusion. She has not been living her life; she has been fulfilling her father's expectations.

As a manifestation of an archetype, the dwarf has both negative and positive aspects. All archetypes do. But until the queen mourns, it is only the negative aspects of the dwarf that are apparent. When the queen breaks through the barrier she has erected between her mind and her heart, uniting her intellect and her emotions, the positive aspect of the dwarf is glimpsed. He tells her what she must do to retain her soul. She must name him.

The act of naming gives one control over what is named. For example, in the Old Testament, Adam gains dominion over the animals by naming them. It was for this reason that, in ancient times, the names of tribal gods were closely guarded secrets. Tribal members feared that if outsiders gained knowledge of their deity's name, they would gain control over the entire tribe. The act of naming also allows for objectivity, for the separation of oneself from what is named. Thus a relationship is allowed to exist where previously there was only an undifferentiated merger.

It is not only in the mythic past that naming is important. It is important even today. For example, when one is affected with a terrible illness, knowing what is physically wrong and being able to name it is somehow affirming. On the other hand, feeling sick and debilitated and not knowing why leaves one in the helpless quandary of a victim. When one can recognize what is wrong and identify the illness by name, one can address the illness, confront it, and hopefully take the proper actions to control it.

In "Rumplestiltskin," it is curious that the dwarf tells the maiden how to control him. This is an important point that we will address shortly.

The queen sends out a messenger, scouring the land for possible names. On two successive nights, the dwarf arrives and she recites possible names for him. But after each recitation the dwarf says, "No, my name is none of these." On the third day the messenger returns, telling how he had crossed a high mountain and entered a wooded area where the foxes and the hares wished him "good night." In that land he had come upon a strange scene, a little man hopping about a fire, singing a song. And in the song the little man stated that his name was Rumplestiltskin. The queen was overjoyed with this serendipitous bit of information.

When the little man arrives for the third and last time, he says, "Now then, queen mother, what is my name?"

"Conrad?" asks the queen.

"No."

"Henry?"

21

> *"No."*
> *"Then your name is Rumplestiltskin."*
> *"The fairies must have told you that," screams the little man in a rage, stomping his right foot so fiercely on the ground that it sinks deeply into the earth, dragging his body after it. Then in his fury, he grabs his left foot with both hands and tears himself completely in half.*

We are told the queen sends a messenger. She does not look to the king for direction as to what she should do. Nor is she attempting to fulfill her father's expectations. At this moment, the queen moves on her own initiative. Propelled by the possibility of redressing the error she had unconsciously committed, the queen moves from passive to active involvement in an attempt to redeem her soul. Up until this point the queen had only concerned herself with being a father's daughter or a king's wife. This is the critical point in the story, because it is here that the queen chooses what she wants. For the first time, she truly is exercising her free will.

The queen enlists the help of a messenger, a man in her service, to do her bidding. In Jungian terms, she is using her active, masculine energy for her own benefit, not for the benefit of the greedy king or to fulfill the expectations of her adoring father. When she begins to utilize this active energy for herself, miraculous things happen. By chance, or fate, or what Jung called synchronicity, the messenger learns the little man's name. It is as if the universe is cooperating with the queen's efforts.

The symbolism of the dwarf is central to this story. The fact that in the fairy tale the dwarf never appears unless the queen is alone suggests that the dwarf represents an aspect of her inner life, an essential element in her psychology. The dwarf is a little man, a male figure and, as such, represents the masculine energy the queen has for herself, in her inner psychological realm. Remember, in the outer world, the world of the father and the world of the king, the queen is honored for doing incredible things. To this outer world, she appears heroic. She displays a personality imbued with the spirit of her father; she is larger than life. However, her inner life, as this story reveals, is dominated by a dwarf, a miniature male who tyrannizes her. In her inner world, she is a helpless maiden. This is the paradox in her life—namely, outwardly the maiden-queen is in control; inwardly, she is a victim.

The dwarf in the fairy tale gained power over the maiden because the maiden wanted to remain her father's daughter. At the crisis point in the tale, the daughter realizes that the cost of continuing in that role is too high. The maiden, now queen, takes the necessary action to free herself from the dwarf's domination. She wins her freedom by naming the dwarf. Once named, the dwarf tears himself in half and disappears. Symbolically, a duality always indicates consciousness. It symbolizes opposition and differentiation. When the dwarf splits himself in two, he shows that he is no longer an unconscious force in the maiden's psyche. The tale states that the dwarf returns to earth, disappears into the ground, indicating that he has returned to his source. The maiden-queen at last is free of the dwarf's influence.

We are not told what happens to the queen after that. That is not the focus of the tale. Rumplestiltskin, as we have noted, describes the dynamics of a father's daughter and focuses on the specific problem of what is required if she is to break her subservience to her father's values and gain her own autonomy. The solution the tale offers is that she must name the dwarf. How would a contemporary father's daughter go about naming the dwarf today? Or for that matter, how do any of us gain freedom from our inner tyrants?

Chapter Four

Naming the Dwarf

In the tale of "Rumplestiltskin," the queen is freed from the tyranny of the dwarf and regains her soul through the act of naming her tyrant. After being named by the queen, the dwarf self-destructs and is no longer a viable presence in the queen's life. The dwarf splits himself in two, suggesting that his secrets have become conscious. But there is still the question of why some individuals have a dwarf in their psyches. And, further, what is it that the dwarf represents? And still further, how do you go about naming a dwarf? To begin answering those questions, it may be helpful to examine individuals who, indeed, do have a dwarf in their psyches. Perhaps such an examination will reveal how one goes about naming a dwarf. It may be that what is discovered may be useful to anyone who seeks to name their inner tyrant. Let me tell you a personal story.

I returned to college in midlife when our oldest daughter was in high school. My determination to earn a master's degree in English and become a teacher was prompted by my desire to help with the financial costs of educating our children. We had six children and I could envision the college tuition bills arriving in a few years at the rate of two or even three at a time. Originally, I thought that I would be in college for a year, two years at the most. As it turned out, my journey through the realms of higher education was much longer than I anticipated.

En route to earning my master's degree in English, I was intro-duced to the writings of Carl Jung and my life turned upside down. Something deep within me responded to Jung's ideas. I felt that Jung was writing about me, that he had seen into my soul even though he had never met me. I knew, with that instinctive knowing one has when one glimpses or experiences one's own truth, that I was to become a Jungian analyst. I also knew, despite my wishful thinking, that the path would be a watercourse way. It would not, could not, be a straight line. It would be difficult, time-consuming, challenging—always challenging—giving me opportunity after opportunity to back away from my goal.

With the dream of becoming a Jungian analyst as my guiding vision, I began my personal analysis. I earned my master's degree in English and continued in graduate school, earning a master's and a doctorate in psychology. Before completing the dissertation for my doctorate, I began my Jungian training. By now, several of our children were in college and the time, energy, and financial constraints were tremendous. I was always under pressure to do more than one thing at a time. I was like the maiden who became the queen in "Rumplestiltskin" completing one impossible task after another. I thought it was by the grace of God that I had progressed as far as I had. I was unlike the "Rumplestiltskin" maiden, however, in that I had never encountered a dwarf. But that was soon to change.

When the time came for me to finish my Jungian training, I had one month free to write my thesis and complete my cases in preparation for my final examination in December. I had completed my doctorate and had completed an internship on August 31st. The completed thesis and cases were to be sent to my examiners by the first of October. If I did not meet this deadline, it would be six months and thousands of additional dollars in expenses before I would have another opportunity to take the final examination. The other factor feeding my determination was the three-hundred mile trip from Detroit to Chicago that I had been making on a weekly basis in order to pursue my Jungian analytical training. I was eager to complete these requirements.

I had given quite a bit of thought to what I wanted to do for my thesis and my cases, but I had not begun writing. I had no other commitments that month, except for seeing a few clients each week. Considering that it was not unusual for a candidate in analytical psychology to take a full year to write a thesis and a few additional months to write up cases, my plan to do both in a little over four weeks could have been viewed as foolhardy or wishful thinking. I saw it as a formidable task but not an impossible one.

I began writing, working, establishing a tight schedule that I knew could work. Then I was besieged by doubts. My inner thoughts questioned what I was doing.

"Will I make a fool of myself?"

"Will I fail?"

"Maybe this is an impossible task."

This was the gist of the dialogue that was going on inside my head. At first, the dialogue started whenever I was tired; then it began to plague me even when I was not tired. One day I stopped and listened carefully to what was being said. I focused my attention, and as I listened, I discovered that I was hearing a voice saying:

"You can't do it."

"You don't have to do this. You don't need it. You could teach."

"You're going to fail, and you're going to be embarrassed."

"Don't do it. If you don't try, you can't fail."

I suddenly realized that it was not "I" talking to myself. I was not the speaker. It was another energy or personality who had entered into a dialogue uninvited by me. What I was hearing was not "I can't do it" but "You can't do it."

I was flabbergasted and shocked, and I wondered: Who is this talking to me? When it finally settled into my brain that this was a personality other than myself, an inner tyrant, I entered into a dialogue with it and began responding to its negative comments.

To the voice that said: "You can't do it," "It's impossible," "Don't humiliate yourself," I consciously and audibly replied: "You may be right. I might fail. But, on the other hand, you may be wrong. I may be able to do it. There is a possibility that I could succeed."

I did not attempt to silence the voice. I listened and countered every negative remark with a positive response. I was consciously separating my ego—that is, my center of will—from that voice. I began to discern that the voice had been speaking in the guise of authority and omniscience, giving pronouncements as if it knew what was going to happen. But as I listened, I realized that the voice did not know.

"We're talking possibilities and probabilities," I began to counter. "I'm choosing to put my energy into the possibility that I can accomplish what I want to accomplish. If I fail, it will be because I fail, not because I didn't try."

It was possible that I could succeed. Admittedly, it would take a great deal of discipline and effort to complete the task on time, but it was possible. Self-defeating behavior, I knew, would at the very least inhibit success and, if it went unchecked, would prevent even the possibility of it. If I had not stopped and dialogued with that inner voice, I might have found myself at the mercy of negative self-concepts and discovered too late that I was fulfilling a self-defeating prophecy.

We played a game, that voice and I. I paid attention whenever doubts began to creep into my thoughts. Time after time I heard the familiar voice of my inner critic. But as I spoke directly to the voice, the voice became silent. "Who are you?" I would ask, recognizing shadings of the voices of individuals from my past. But it was not the voice of one particular person, it was more of a conglomerate. I persisted. Each time I heard my inner, self-defeating comments, I would ask, "Who are you? You're so familiar to me. It seems that you've been with me for a long time."

Gradually, the voice took on a form. It was not a parental figure or a school teacher or anyone I had ever encountered. As I finally discovered, the voice belonged to a dwarf. I was surprised but somehow not surprised. I never actually named the dwarf, but I knew who he was — yes, it was a he — and he knew that I knew him. There was no more sliding, hiding from me.

On one occasion when I was struggling to write, he became so vociferous that I ordered him, "Sit over there on that chair and be quiet. You're not going to drain off any more of my energy. I am going to focus on doing what I have to do." And I felt enormous relief.

Later, I thought, "Thank God no one's around hearing me talk to a dwarf that no one can see but me." But my dwarf, I knew, was real — at least for me.

My dwarf reappeared periodically, sneakily, but I could always catch him when I realized self-defeating thoughts were in my head. Incidentally, I did finish the writing on time.

In the course of my work and in workshops that I have given, I have talked to many women and found that dwarfs are common inner tyrants for father's daughters who, like the "Rumplestiltskin" maiden, are striving to achieve in their father's world. However, not all father's daughters have dwarfs. The inner tyrant might take the form of a witch or some other archetype. And it is not only women who have dwarfs and witches. Men can have them too. However, regardless of what personification the inner tyrant takes and regardless of whether you are a woman or a man, the steps required to free yourself from the tyrant's control are the same as those required to name the dwarf.

1. Listen to the voice; do not ignore it. As you listen carefully and observe what is going on in your mind, your emotions, and your body, you will discover that a mood, a thought, or a feeling will precede the voice. Pay attention. Do not attempt to change what you are experiencing. Do not try to shut it off or make it go away. This shift in attitude from trying to deny or control

what is going on within you to merely observing it is really a major shift. This change in perspective, the change into the role of the observer, moves you out of being a victim. When you change your attitude, you are no longer controlled by, or at the mercy of, what the inner voice is saying to you. In other words, you are breaking the old patterns.

2. Accurately hear what the voice is saying. Listen carefully and realize that it is not you talking to yourself. Hear the voice say, for example, "You can't do that," or "You shouldn't be doing that; that's not right." Hear the voice speaking to you in the second person. It is not you thinking to yourself in a first-person voice and saying, "I can't do that." Pay attention to what else is going on in your body. What mood, emotion, or self-doubt is connected to the voice?

   One client, a man who had been abused physically, sexually, and emotionally in childhood, went through the steps of naming his tyrant. His was not a dwarf, however; it felt more like a boa constrictor, which tightened its hold on him whenever he displayed any sign of life. It was as slippery, however, as my dwarf in not wanting to be seen directly. The man observed that a feeling would come upon him, and then he would wish that he were dead. Careful observation of what was happening revealed that the first thought that entered his head was "I wish you were dead" not "I wish I was dead." And in recalling his history, the fact that he was conceived in premarital sex and his conception forced his parents—two members of an extremely repressive religious group—to get married, it made sense that his deepest imprinting was the fact that he was not a wanted child. As he integrated the fact that his mother and his father did not want the responsibility of a baby nor the shame that he brought them, he recognized that he had internalized their wish that he did not exist. Hearing the voice accurately and admitting aloud that he was glad to be alive changed his attitude. He moved from the position of victim and began to take control of his life.

3. Address the voice. Consciously dialogue with it whenever self-doubts, guilt, or self-defeating thoughts enter your mind. Respond to each doubt, guilt, or negative comment with a positive

remark that counters the negativity you experience. If the voice says, for example, "You're being selfish. You're only thinking of yourself," respond with something like, "I am. It's time I thought about myself. If I don't think about myself, who will?"

4. See what image the voice takes. You may be able to recognize the voice as coming from a dwarf, a witch, or a dirty old man right from the beginning. However, it may be that the voice will not be personified until later.

5. From the position of your own authority, state that you are making a choice. Acknowledge what the voice says but confront the voice with the truth that what is being spoken is only a probability; it is not an accurate prophecy. Make your choice as to what you want to do. Speak from the position that you are the choice-maker. To the inner comment that you are being selfish, for example, you might respond, "I'm sure from your perspective, it looks that way. From my perspective, it's time I thought about myself. I choose to put myself first."

6. Take responsibility for what you choose. For example, "If I fail, it will be because I failed, not because I didn't try." Or, "I choose to do this because I want to do it. I do not do this to deliberately hurt anyone's feelings. If someone's feelings are hurt (e.g., your mother's or your lover's) because I do this, so be it. I'll live with the consequences."

The tyranny of the dwarf is an inner tyranny. Every person I have encountered, without exception, if she or he is honest, will admit to having an inner tyrant who induces guilt or shame or self-doubt. This inner tyrant limits the person's potential by keeping him or her fearful— fearful of being embarrassed, fearful of being seen as imperfect, fearful of being shamed for being flawed, or fearful of ceasing to exist if he or she does not conform.

For the "Rumplestiltskin" maiden, the inner tyrant, the dwarf, kept her striving to fulfill her father's image of who she was and prevented her from discovering her true Self. The maiden did not know herself as an independent, autonomous human being. She existed as daughter, wife, and then mother; in all instances, she served as handmaiden to the lord—the masculine, patriarchal culture. To the outer world she appeared successful and accomplished. In her inner world she was ruled by the archetype of the dwarf.

What does the symbol of the dwarf represent? In ancient mythology, the dwarf is often pictured as the companion of the Great Mother or the Great Goddess. Dwarfs were depicted as working as miners in the mountains or in subterranean passages. As companions of the Great Mother, the dwarfs represented her masculine counterpart.

The Great Goddess religions did not have a male counterpart for the goddess who was her equal. The goddess always had a diminished male partner. There has been much discussion lately about the partnership model of relationships that existed during the eras of Great Mother worship (Eisler 1986). The fact remains, however, regardless of the discussion, that there was not equality between women and men or between the Great Goddess and her consort. For example, the Great Mother could have a son-lover as a companion, and he would be sacrificed annually and replaced by a new son-lover (Graves 1948). It appears that the more powerful the goddess was, the more diminished her male counterpart would be. This would account for the fact that in the ancient religions where the goddess was all-powerful, her masculine companion was often a dwarf, a "little man," a manikin, less than human.

In the tale of "Rumplestiltskin," the dwarf splits in half after he is named and sinks into the earth, into matter, into the mother. His power as tyrant has been replaced by new masculine energy in the form of the queen's messenger. Here at last is masculine energy in the service of the queen. Although the fairy tale does not reveal a partnership of equals, it does reveal how the queen's inner masculine energy, what Jung called her *animus*, has developed from a dwarf into an adult messenger. "Rumplestiltskin," in true fairy tale fashion, concerns one particular psychological problem that an individual may encounter as she moves toward increased consciousness. Specifically, it relates how freedom from an inner tyrant can be attained. The tale is told from the perspective of a woman's journey and it is a particular type of woman, a father's daughter, who is central to the tale. However, naming one's inner tyrant is a task everyone must undertake.

In continuing our examination of father's daughters, we can legitimately ask: What are the dynamics operating in a woman's psyche when a dwarf rules her inner world? I think it is relevant to utilize Jung's theories on masculine and feminine energies as we search for an answer to this question.

30

It is imperative that the terms *masculine* and *feminine* be clarified. *Masculine* and *feminine*, in this context, are symbolic terms. I am relying on symbolic language to describe and explain the two different energies that are present in each human being. I am not implying gender when I use these words. I am not stating that only men have masculine energy and only women have feminine energy. Both energies exist in each and every human being. Admittedly, it is difficult to stay with the symbolic, and the words *masculine* and *feminine* are often problematic.

In workshops when I have focused on the topic of masculine and feminine energies, I have had women become so angry with me that they have walked out of my presentation. I have also had men interrupt me when I am lecturing and challenge what I have labeled as feminine, declaring that what I called feminine was a part of their personality. In such instances the symbolic had become concrete. So I urge you to stay with the symbolic as we move through this discussion of psychological dynamics.

Jung shocked his world in the early twentieth century when he declared that men had a feminine side and women a masculine side. Globally, he described masculine energies as *Logos* and feminine energies as *Eros*. *Logos*, meaning word, speech, discourse, and reason, relates to logic, meaning, thought, and abstraction. *Eros*, meaning love, connects with eroticism and sexuality and refers to relatedness, relationship, connectedness, and belonging.

The different energies operating in the human psyche have been recognized by many other people. Otto Rank, for example, called these two different energies *drives*. He distinguished between the drive toward separation and the drive toward union. In Rank's system, the human dilemma was of being forever caught between the desire for freedom and the desire to belong. In other words, he saw humans as struggling between the pull toward independence and the pull toward relating within a group. Rank saw the drives as equal forces within the human psyche.

Jung struggled to give feminine energies equal status with masculine energies. He did not always succeed. In subtle ways, the feminine energies were diminished. However, Jung used the Taoist symbol of yin and yang to illustrate what he meant by the relationship between masculine and feminine. This ancient symbol, depicting a human being as one totality with two inseparable parts, did value both energies equally. The yin-yang represents the integration of the feminine and masculine principles into a related whole, with each energetic force dependent upon the other. The seed of yin, the feminine, lies within the fullness of yang, the masculine, and the seed of yang within the fullness of yin. It is impossible for either yin or yang to exist by itself.

The yin-yang relationship is like breathing. Inhaling and exhaling comprise a rhythmic unity. The feminine part is the inhalation with the breath coming in and going down. The masculine energy is the exhalation with the breath going up and out. Inhalation and exhalation are inseparable and they exist as equals. The recognition of breath as symbolizing the unity of masculine and feminine energies is almost universal. It is taught in traditions from the East to the West, from the Buddhist to the Native American. Both masculine and feminine energies are required and are operative in life at all times. There is always a balance, seen or unseen.

Jung looked at the physical body for examples of how nature maintains a balance and discussed how nature relies on compensatory mechanisms. For example, he drew on the homeostasis of the body to explain compensation. In homeostasis, the inner temperature of the vital organs is maintained by the blood flow. If the internal temperature drops, blood is withdrawn from the extremities. The hands and feet may feel the cold, but the internal organs are warmed. The reverse is also true: if the temperature rises for the internal organs, blood circulates more rapidly around the body, giving off heat, causing skin temperatures to rise. Hands and feet are hot but the internal organs are cooled.

Jung maintained that nature followed a similar process in the psychological realm, maintaining a psychic homeostasis, as it were. To keep the balance of psychic energies, nature enforces a compensatory relationship between one's outer and one's inner life. For example, a one-sidedness in an individual's conscious attitude or behavior would be compensated in the unconscious by the opposite attitude or behavior. In this way a balance is maintained. The more one-sided the conscious attitude, the more extreme the compensation in the individual's unconscious.

Both masculine and feminine energies are required and are operative in life. If one is repressed in the outer life, it will be exaggerated in the inner life. The aim, as Jung saw it, was to have harmony and balance between the feminine and the masculine, both in the inner world and in the outer world.

One of the most helpful examinations of the interrelatedness of the masculine and feminine energies, from a Jungian perspective, was offered by the Jungian analyst Miriam Freitas (1981). I offer her conceptualization and my subsequent theoretical formulations to show the foundation of my thoughts regarding the dynamics of the father's daughter.

In Freitas's conceptualization, the feminine and masculine energies are referred to by the Jungian terms *Eros* and *Logos*. However, she continues beyond Jung's definition to include the negative aspects of each of those forces. As shown in figure 1 on the following page, the positive side of Eros is relatedness or connectedness; the negative side of Eros is chaos or nondifferentiation. In today's terminology, the negative aspect could be described as an absence of boundaries. In regard to Logos, Freitas defined the positive attributes as independence or differentiation and the negative attributes as alienation and isolation.

What becomes apparent in Freitas's schema is that the negative aspects occur when the positive aspects become extreme. Too much relatedness, for example, can result in a lack of differentiation between oneself and another. Too much separateness and independence, on the other hand, can lead to alienation and isolation—a sense of not belonging.

The two principles—the feminine and masculine energies—in their positive aspects are not opposites of each other; they are different energies, complementary energies. The oppositions are revealed when the negative aspects come into play. In figure 2 on the following page, the opposite of relatedness and connectedness is alienation and isolation. This means that the bright side of Eros is opposed by the dark side of Logos. Conversely, separateness and independence—the positive side of Logos—are opposed by chaos and nondifferentiation—the negative side of Eros.

There is an implied system of checks and balances in Freitas's schema that is congruent with Jung's ideas of compensatory functions within the psyche. In order for the feminine and the masculine energies to remain positive, each must incorporate some of the other. Eros, as relatedness, will move into merger and chaos without the limitation of logical delineation. Likewise, Logos, as independence, separates into isolation without the expansion of connectedness.

Another way to distinguish between feminine and masculine energies is to call the feminine energies *being* energies and the masculine energies *becoming* energies. On page 35, figure 3—which incorporates the concepts of Jung, Freitas, Rank, and others—reveals that a relationship can only occur when there is a union of separate, equally positive

	Positive Aspects	**Negative Aspects**
Feminine *Eros*	Relatedness Connectedness	Chaos Nondifferentiation
Masculine *Logos*	Independence Differentiation	Alienation Isolation

Fig. 1. The positive and negative attributes of Eros and Logos, according to Freitas (1981)

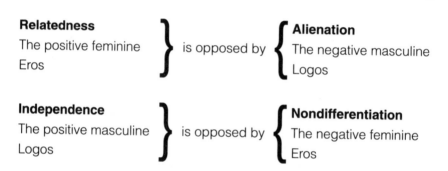

Relatedness
The positive feminine
Eros
} is opposed by { **Alienation**
The negative masculine
Logos

Independence
The positive masculine
Logos
} is opposed by { **Nondifferentiation**
The negative feminine
Eros

Fig. 2. The oppositions between Eros (feminine) and Logos (masculine), according to Freitas (1981)

energies. Relationship implies equality. Anything else is symbiosis or an interaction of domination and submission.

When the feminine and the masculine energies relate to each other in a positive way, something greater than the sum of their parts is manifested. Jung maintained that this coming together of one's feminine and masculine energies—this inner marriage or what he called *coniunctio*—was necessary before one's unique personality could be realized. Freitas's conceptualization begins to suggest what that marriage would look like.

What becomes apparent is that for a relationship to occur, positive aspects of both the feminine and the masculine energies must be involved. The interrelatedness of these two energies is such that when

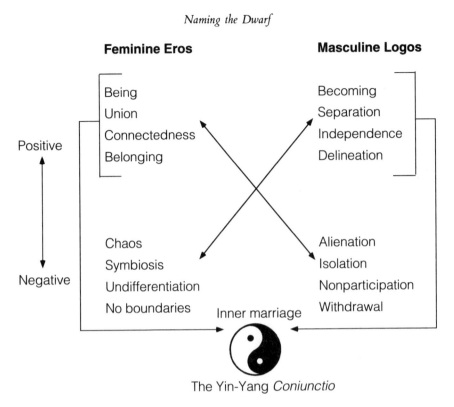

Feminine Eros   **Masculine Logos**

Positive

Being   Becoming
Union   Separation
Connectedness   Independence
Belonging   Delineation

Chaos   Alienation
Symbiosis   Isolation
Undifferentiation   Nonparticipation
No boundaries   Withdrawal

Negative

Inner marriage

The Yin-Yang *Coniunctio*

Fig. 3. An inner marriage between equals requires positive aspects of both the feminine and the masculine energies

one of them is negative, the other is also negative; it cannot be positive. This means that if negative masculine energy is dominating one's behavior, negative feminine energy will also be present.

This schema offers an overall view of feminine and masculine dynamics operating within an individual's psyche. In a way, it is too simplistic because feminine and masculine energies operate in two arenas in our lives. In the outer world, their interaction determines how we relate to other individuals and to our environment. In the inner world, their interaction determines how we relate to ourselves. A compensatory relationship exists between the two worlds as far as how the feminine and the masculine energies operate. This may become more obvious as we continue our quest to discover why some individuals have a dwarf in their psyches.

In the fairy tale "Rumplestiltskin," there was a conscious overvaluing of masculine energies by the maiden. Her outer dynamics were skewed toward becoming and achieving as she spun the straw into gold. She did not question her role as daughter to her father or, later, wife to the king; she always did what she was told and kept herself subordinate to the masculine values of the patriarchy. Symbiotically, she held those values as her own.

In her conscious, outer life, the "Rumplestiltskin" maiden had a masculine-feminine interaction in which the masculine energies dominated. This interaction could be symbolized as the masculine (God the Father, Zeus, or the king who expects to be obeyed unquestioningly) dominating the submissive feminine (the daughter, the servant, the handmaiden who would give her life, her body, her energy to perpetuate her father's values). Thus the maiden's dynamics would look something like the diagram in figure 4.

The relationship between masculine and feminine in the maiden's unconscious or inner life would compensate for her outer attitude and behavior. This means several things. First, the greater the elevation of "father" in the conscious, physical realm, the more the masculine is diminished in the unconscious, inner world. That is to say, a Zeus-like energy in the outer world calls forth a little man or dwarf in the inner world. Further, the elevation of the masculine in the outer world—with the feminine subordinated or dominated as handmaiden or servant—is countered by the elevation of the feminine in the inner world. God the Father is balanced by God the Mother, so that the patriarchal Godhead is matched by the Great Goddess. A further compensation or completion occurs because the Great Goddess complements or fulfills the daughter, the handmaiden. The goddess is great while the maiden is small.

When both the inner and the outer dynamics are analyzed, it is apparent that there is an equality between the feminine and the masculine energies. The dwarf-Great Goddess relationship mirrors the daughter-God the Father dyad. Both are archetypal patterns. Together they form a whole.

The inner world compensates and complements the outer world, balancing the feminine and masculine energies. Jung did not write about the inner and outer worlds of behavior as often as he wrote about conscious and unconscious behavior. But people today are much more aware of themselves and their complexities than people were at the beginning of this century when Jung began writing. Today it is not uncommon for individuals to realize there can be a difference between their outer behavior and their inner sense of self. They recognize the

	Unconscious The Inner World	**Conscious** The Outer World
Dominant Energy	Feminine Great Mother	Masculine God the Father
Submissive Energy	Masculine dwarf	Feminine her father's daughter as handmaiden or helper

Fig. 4. The "Rumplestiltskin" maiden's masculine and feminine energies

discrepancy between how they appear to others and how they experience themselves. There are women, for example, who are extremely successful in the professional world and project an image of self-assured competency yet who feel insecure and shamed in their inner, private worlds (McGrew 1989).

Whether we refer to the inner and outer worlds or to conscious and unconscious behavior, the balancing act of feminine and masculine energies is not simple. These energies are equally powerful in the human psyche, and their multifaceted relationship is a dynamic one, not static.

In "Rumplestiltskin," the maiden shifts out of her subservient role and assumes her own power by naming the dwarf. By this act and her assumption of power in the outer world, the maiden brings about a completely different configuration in all aspects of her feminine and masculine energies. She is bringing the masculine and feminine energies into balance in her outer and her inner worlds. In each person's life, the feminine-masculine relationship can be radically altered as the individual gains in self-awareness and incorporates the awareness into behavior. For the "Rumplestiltskin" maiden the change began when she realized she was losing her soul. For her and for every father's daughter, indeed for every human being, the point of change is always the point where one is out of balance. It is the point where weakness exists, where what has been neglected must be revitalized.

For father's daughters, the moment of possible change arrives when they realize that their positive father complex has turned negative. They recognize that they are out of balance. Perhaps if we look a

	Unconscious The Inner World	**Conscious** The Outer World
Dominant Energy	Feminine wicked witch	Masculine puer or one of the boys
Submissive Energy	Masculine dirty old man or wolf in sheep's clothing	Feminine delightful daughter or playmate

Fig. 5. The dynamics when the inner tyrant is a witch

little closer at the psyche of the father's daughter, examining how she lives her life, we may get some clues as to how the imbalance occurs. (Incidentally, the configuration described here for a father's daughter who has not yet named the dwarf may also apply to a man who is living his outward life as a Zeus-like father or king.)

What about women who have a witch as an inner tyrant? What do their dynamics look like? In my experience, such women are usually charming, attractive, and maidenly. Almost without exception, their fathers can be classified as boyish men or, in the Jungian term, *puers* — that is, Peter Pans, men who do not want to grow up. These are men who do not take direct control. They do control, but they do not take control openly. They are often passive-aggressive, providing financial support but withdrawing from family interactions. Sometimes these fathers are alcoholics. The daughter is a delightful playmate, aligning with the father's spirit. She does not want control either. Often she wants someone to take care of her. These women usually like nice clothes and often have a fondness for jewelry.

The compensation for the daughter who does not want control is the witch who does want control and uses any means, magical or otherwise, to attain it. The masculine counterpart in the unconscious would be the complement of the witch: a wolf in sheep's clothing or a dirty old man. This inner masculine is like a snake in the grass, a sneaky counterpart to the naive Peter Pan.

A father's daughter who has a witch as an inner tyrant faces the same challenge as the "Rumplestiltskin" maiden. Namely, she must determine what is right for her and take the actions necessary to move from being a daughter—in this case, a playmate—to being a woman in charge of her own destiny. The particular tasks she faces may differ from those faced by the "Rumplestiltskin" maiden, but the techniques she uses are identical. Here my focus is on father's daughters who are like the "Rumplestiltskin" maiden. For those women who have a witch as an inner tyrant, "Hansel and Gretel" could be used instead for archetypal amplification.

Chapter Five

Understanding
The Hero Within Is Without

The fairy tale of "Rumplestiltskin" does not describe the day-to-day activities of the maiden/queen. Only the bare essentials are given, and they are given symbolically. Yet from these bare essentials the "Rumplestiltskin" maiden is revealed as the prototype for a particular kind of woman. Her sisters, who are father's daughters like she is, are handmaidens to the lord, serving their master — whether he be father, husband, church, or society — by being accomplished in the patriarchal world. The "Rumplestiltskin" maiden is the one who is able to spin straw into gold. It is she who, by the simple act of spinning, takes the mundane and commonplace and transforms it into something special and valuable. It is she who is the accomplished one, the focused one, the one who gets things done despite the overwhelming odds and the cost to her inner life. The fairy tale depicts the role that these father's daughters seek to perfect.

For the contemporary woman who is a father's daughter, her mantle of accomplishments, adorned with the fruits of her active, masculine energy (awards, degrees, achievements) hides and protects an inner world where masculine energy in the service of her true self is diminished and dwarfed. She has the same dynamics as the "Rumplestiltskin" maiden in that although she may appear heroic to the outer world, in her inner world, the hero is absent.

As noted previously, masculine energy (as well as feminine energy) occurs in both the outer and the inner world of every human being. In setting out his conceptualization of the human psyche, Jung said that a woman's conscious energy was feminine. It was embodied in her female form and was congruent with her sexuality. Her masculine energy, labeled her *animus*, was contrasexual and resided in the unconscious. Jung stated that a woman had an animus and a man did not. A man's masculine energy, according to Jung, was conscious, embodied in his physical form. His contrasexual energy, his feminine side, was personified in his dreams and his unconscious by his *anima*, an inner feminine figure holding the man's receptivity and creativity.

For me, Jung's terms of *animus* and *anima* are confusing. They were probably appropriate terms a generation or two ago, when people were not so aware of the complexity of their own natures. At that time, men were as shocked to learn they had a feminine side as women were to learn of their masculine aspect. I prefer to let the terms *animus* and *anima* reside in the past because they are not helpful for me. I feel they are used to make artificial distinctions, so that feminine energies, for example, are discussed differently depending on whether they are manifested in a woman or in a man's anima. But are they really different? And does it make a difference, in discussing masculine energies, whether these occur in a man or a woman? I think not.

There are men who are out of touch with their masculinity as well as women who are distanced from their femininity. It becomes confusing for me to talk about the anima and the animus with these individuals. It is also difficult to talk about the animus when describing the dynamics of father's daughters. So with a nod of appreciation to Jung for undercutting the belief that biology was destiny, I will set *animus* and *anima* aside. I prefer to use the terms *masculine energy* or *feminine energy* regardless of the gender of the individual being discussed.

What becomes apparent in women who, like the "Rumplestiltskin" maiden, are handmaidens of the lord is that they have a peculiar imbalance of feminine and masculine energies. In consciousness, in their outer lives, these women have devalued their feminine energies. For them, the feminine is subservient to the masculine, not its equal. They concretize that subservience in their lives by remaining daughters and never becoming equals to their "fathers." Just as they devalue the feminine, they overvalue the masculine.

When father's daughters embody heroism in their lives, the heroism is not for themselves. For example, one father's daughter might be a pediatric nurse championing the cause of the young children in her care, unafraid of challenging male or female authority figures. She can and does fight for the rights of others, especially when they cannot fight for themselves, and she is effective in doing this. However, this same woman finds surrender or receptivity difficult. She can do for others but is awkward when it comes to having others do for her. Rarely will she ask for help, even if it means pushing herself to the limits of her physical ability. Inwardly she would like to surrender, give up being in charge, and relax. Yet she is so adept at masking her inner feelings that other people view her as strong, competent, and able to take care of herself. Active, masculine energy used in the service of others is well developed in these particular father's daughters. Their heroic efforts are highly visible, but their inward hero is nonexistent.

Many writers have considered the development of a woman's masculine energies. Carol Pearson, in *The Hero Within* (1986), examines the archetypes of orphan, martyr, hero, warrior, and magician, noting how they affect a woman's behavior. Polly Young-Eisendrath and Florence Wiedemann, in their book, *Female Authority* (1987), observe from a Jungian perspective what it means for a woman to embrace her masculinity for herself, wedding it to her femininity and finding her authentic voice. Other writers who have explored the female psyche include Laura McGrew (1989), who analyzes the differences between a woman's public life and her private self, and Carolyn Stevens who, in her work on the gendered self (1985), maintains that the soul image, the Self, in a woman is female. All these works are helpful in understanding a woman's psyche.

I have no intention of replicating what has been written already. What I am hoping to do here is to demonstrate a way for women to break out of the old roles, the old personae, the old myths and patterns, and to discover their true personalities, their true selves. To illustrate the transformations that occur in this process, I will confine myself to the stories of father's daughters who are like the "Rumplestiltskin" maiden. However, women who are not father's daughters and perhaps even men may find the techniques outlined here useful in discovering or, more accurately, recovering their true selves.

Before she named the dwarf, the "Rumplestiltskin" maiden was out of balance in regard to her feminine and masculine energies. She was caught in a repetitive cycle, striving to incarnate the myth of being her father's daughter. This myth ruled her life and continues to rule the lives of many women today. To better understand what it means to have the myth of "Her Father's Daughter" ruling one's life, let us look at the psychological dynamics underlying the day-to-day lives of contemporary father's daughters. For those familiar with the Star Maiden Circle as explained in *Dancing the Wheel of Psychological Types* (Loomis 1990), what follows will be recognized as the movement called the Circle of Foxes.

First of all, a woman like the maiden in "Rumplestiltskin" has found her identity in life by being her father's daughter and serving as hand-maiden to the lord. She begins with serving her personal father; later "father" becomes any male-dominated institution of religion, culture, or state. Being her father's daughter permeates and controls her entire life. It is the ideal she strives to maintain.

All of the experiences she encounters in life are viewed from the perspective of the father's daughter. She feels she is to be of service to others, to be responsible, to be dependable. There are certain things expected of father's daughters, certain things she is to do and certain things she is not to do. She does not cross the line. Her life is lived in a co-dependent relationship that is familiar to her. Her sense of personal empowerment is dependent upon her father, upon the patriarchy and what the patriarchy values. She excels, becoming the queen of her domain, whatever it may be. It may be in a marriage and motherhood. It may be the corporate world. But whatever she actualizes in her life, it is within the restraints determined by the "fathers." She lacks true em-powerment because she only actualizes what is acceptable to the patri-archy.

Implicitly or explicitly, father—the personal father or the collective father—defines her behavior. She conducts herself in accordance to the moral tenets of church or state law and feels guilty when she breaks these rules. The moral behavior the rules and laws delineate are de-signed to keep her in a subordinate role, and they always extend to her sexuality, to controlling her body, and to repressing her sexual behav-ior.

As long as she is following father's guidelines, she does not have to think for herself. She is convinced that the values she holds are correct. Her life is secure and predictable. Her esteem for the patriarchy and her love for her father are unshakable. With the moral certitude that she is right, that she knows the truth, she may become a stalwart supporter of her church or temple. She may become active in a political party, trying to sway others to her point of view. She knows her way is the correct way and regards individuals with other perceptions, other realities, other beliefs as mistaken, misguided, or misinformed.

All of the choices and decisions she makes are in accord with the values of the fathers and are intended to perpetuate the status quo. She strives for perfection in the role she plays, and in her focused intent, she is blind to any other way of being. She may talk about her free will and believe she is thinking for herself. However, she is caught in an illusion. She is following her father's guidelines in the priorities she establishes for herself and the decisions she makes. If she truly were left to her own devices, she would be as nondifferentiating as the Great Mother, equally valuing a flea and an elephant.

She is living out her father's expectations of who she is and who she should be. It has not even crossed her mind to imagine what life would be like if she relinquished her role as her father's daughter. Secure in her tight little world, she would find a world without father unthinkably frightening.

All of her self-concepts center on being a daughter, a female with less power than father. She does not define herself as being a woman who is the equal to her father, and in her inner world, the feminine side of the Divine is absent. There are no peers for the patriarchal gods. Staying attached to being her father's daughter, content to be the power behind the throne, guarantees affirmation from her father and from the patriarchal institutions. She is not willing to surrender this affirmation, to risk the loss of her father's love. She feels she has nothing within her to replace his love because she has not yet found a way to love herself.

This is the pattern that the father's daughter, the woman like the maiden in our fairy tale, repeats and repeats. She is rewarded for her behavior, for being a daughter to the patriarchy. She never thinks about changing. Why should she? Everything is going along smoothly. It is not a strain for her to abide by the rules and laws governing her life. It is not until she realizes the exorbitant cost she will have to pay to continue in the old, familiar ways that she contemplates change. The moment she refuses to passively surrender her soul, she challenges, for the first time, the rules and laws enforced by the dwarf.

In the fairy tale, it was the dwarf who exacted payment from the maiden. She had to pay the dwarf in order to remain a favored daughter, playing the role, perpetuating the myth. For all of us, women and men alike, the dwarf represents that relentless inner dialogue that always points out what we should be doing, how we should be doing it, and how guilty we will feel if we do not align with the voice's dictates.

We always have a choice at each critical point. The queen in the fairy tale, for example, could have surrendered her soul instead of aligning with her emotions and confronting the dwarf. What is for one person too high a price, another may pay. Each father's daughter, and in fact each human being, is given opportunity after opportunity to stop and consider the price being paid to perpetuate the myth. For some women, the tribute being exacted, the one that finally forces her to reflect on how she is living her life, may be a physical illness so severe that her life is threatened. Yet the woman still has a choice. She can change or she can die. It is a critical point. If she decides to change, she must realize fully, just as the queen did with her weeping, what she has paid through the years to maintain the myth.

Until the moment when the maiden/queen acknowledges that she can no longer pay the price demanded of her, she has been overidentified with masculine values. At the point when she undertakes to name the dwarf, she shifts from being a child to being a woman and simultaneously shifts from being a victim—at the mercy of what the fathers wanted from her—to being an observer, a survivor. From there, she shifts to being in control of her own life, making her own decisions, and taking responsibility for them. She does not look to the fathers to tell her what to do. At this moment, and not until this moment, the woman has free will. She has broken the pattern. Until now, all of her choices were predetermined by the myth she was living. Now she has changed her myth. No longer will she be contained within and defined by the myth of the father's daughter.

Chapter Six

The False Self
The Root of Shame

What is it that leads a father's daughter to live her life as a daughter and not as an empowered woman? Why does she live the illusion that she cannot be mistress of her own fate? For that matter, why do any of us live our lives incarnating a myth that limits our potential by keeping us locked into old patterns? Many hypotheses could be generated in an attempt to answer these questions. What follows in this chapter are my musings regarding the dynamics operating in the psyche of a father's daughter—dynamics that reflect a human condition, dynamics of what I believe is a universal human experience.

In nature, when a seed is planted, whether by the intention of a human being or the grander intention of Grandmother Earth, it remains in darkness until the warmth of spring signals "It's time," and then a shoot goes forth stretching for the light. The initial swelling burst of life is fed by the resources within the seed itself. And then a second shoot goes forth; this one moves downward into the earth. As the growth continues, each upward surge is counterbalanced by an unseen movement in the dark. A network of roots develops, sustaining the visible plant. The outward canopy is matched by the hidden root structure in the earth. Without that hidden, unseen growth, the plant—whether a marigold or an oak tree—would not survive.

Stretching for the light, while important for the plant, is not enough by itself. If the outer growth is cut or accidentally broken, the roots send another shoot, another life energy, pulsing toward the light. However, if the root structure is destroyed, the plant dies.

The darkness of the earth also nurtures and protects the roots, the rhizomes, and the bulbs once they have been established. In the fall and winter they lie hidden, incubating, waiting for spring and the beginning of a new growing cycle.

In a pattern similar to that of a plant, the psychological or spiritual life of a human being follows the symmetry of seen and unseen development. This dual movement exists from the beginning of life. On the one hand, there is an awareness of the outer world, a striving for the light, as one seeks pleasure, adaptation, and survival. On the other hand, there is an awareness of the inner world, a reaching into one's core toward the darkness of the unseen, hidden mystery. This hidden growth is as vital to the life of an individual as the root structure is to the life of a plant.

A child is birthed out of perfection. She is conceived and created out of a perfect blending of feminine and masculine energies. Her physical body—the soma—is the result of the genetic coding carried by the particular ovum and the particular sperm—the feminine and the masculine—that have united to form her. The child's psychological or spiritual body—the psyche—is also birthed from a harmonic balance of feminine and masculine energies. In its completeness, the child's psyche mirrors the beauty and majesty of the Divine. Her core, as Carl Jung saw it, is the Self, the image of God within. The Divine, whether it is the image within or the power without, in my view, holds feminine and masculine energies in harmony and balance. It is from the polarization of these two different energies that the mystical, magical transcendence is created.

The child is born out of this perfection, a miracle born from the spirit, from the majesty and awesomeness of the Divine. She enters this physical plane "trailing clouds of glory," as the poet William Wordsworth so beautifully stated, and these "clouds of glory" connect her to the unknowable mystery. She is a child of the Divine. But she is not aware of her spiritual connection to the Divine, not conscious of her glory.

At birth, the child is born into a Garden of Eden and she is at one with her magnificence. It is necessary for her to separate from the garden if she is ever to gain consciousness of who she truly is. She must break free and move out of that uroboric container if she is ever to become a reflective atom of the universe. As she is expelled from the garden, the child, "trailing clouds of glory," forgets how wonderful she is. Day to day, as she lives in the physical world, the memory of her glory fades, until finally the day arrives—probably before she enters school—when the little child no longer remembers her beauty, no longer remembers that she truly is full of wonder.

It is impossible for the child to sustain her oneness with the Divine because from the moment of birth, she is living a paradox. Psychologi-

47

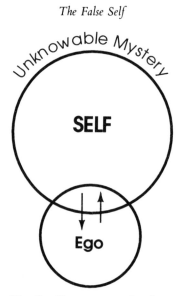

Fig. 6. The ego emerging from
the Self "trailing clouds of glory"

cally and spiritually, the child contains the grandeur and the majesty of
the sacred mystery, "the clouds of glory." However, physically, the child
is helpless, small, weak, and totally dependent upon others for survival.
Her cognitive thought processes have not developed to the stage of
maturity that would allow her to handle paradox. The helplessness she
experiences as she seeks to survive – doing what she must to adapt to
the demands and expectations of parents and society – conflicts with the
majesty of her true spirit. Unable, because of her physical limitations, to
access and manifest her greatness, unable to be autonomous – the quality her greatness bestows upon her – the child experiences inadequacy.
She feels she is not good enough, she is flawed; something about her is
insufficient. In her psyche, the roots of shame take form.

The greatness lying within, the greatness that is her birthright, is
denied. Her physical and mental limitations engulf her with feelings of
helplessness, overriding her greatness. Her greatness now is experienced as an illusion. It cannot be true. If the little girl still has an inkling
of her majesty, it is experienced as flawed. Her helplessness shames
her and she blames herself. It is her fault that she is helpless. The flaws
are hers; it is her insufficiency, her inadequacy. Spiritually she knows
she is supposed to be independent, she is supposed to be autonomous.

The child does not go through a logical thought process to arrive at

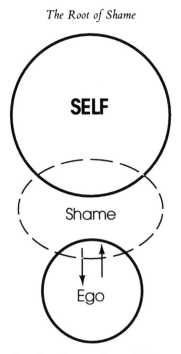

Fig. 7. The ego forgetting its
connection to the Self and
replacing the authentic Self with
the illusory shameful self

this self-blaming, self-shaming conclusion. In infancy and early child-hood, the child is not capable of thinking logically. She experiences the helplessness in her body. She experiences in her body the shame of being flawed, and the shame is configured with embarrassment and humiliation. It is not only father's daughters who experience this shame. All daughters and, in fact, all infants suffer through this process.

Psychological literature is replete with case studies and theories focusing on the trauma and shame individuals experience when they are caught in a conflict that they are helpless to change. When the conflict is extreme and chronic—for example, in instances of childhood physical or sexual abuse—the result may be learned helplessness, borderline per-sonality, or multiple personality disorder. When the conflict is acute—a one-time event or an event of short duration, such as occur during war or physical conflict—post-traumatic stress disorder is often the out-come. In all of these conflicting experiences, the individuals blame themselves for being helpless, for not being able to effect a change in the outcome. The shame and guilt these individuals experience are overwhelming.

These well-documented instances of not being able to exercise one's free will, of not being able to be autonomous, are extreme manifestations, I believe, of the fundamental conflict that each human child endures. Each child experiences helplessness. The physical body into which she is born assures that will be the case. The child's free will is blocked by her physical limitations. Whether mild or severe, the inner conflict that occurs in each child is generated by the paradox between physical limitations and spiritual greatness. The lack of autonomy, the experience of helplessness when one does not wish to be helpless, forces one to experience the tension between those built-in opposites. This tension may generate anger and rage but, underlying these emotions, each child experiences shame over her limitations, her imperfections, her helplessness.

It has been suggested that shame may be the primary cause of emotional distress in our time (Karen 1992). It is my contention that shame has been the primary cause of emotional distress throughout all time and continues to be so. It is also my contention that shame is the result of a universal experience, the experience of the basic paradox of physical helplessness and spiritual greatness.

The roots of shame begin with the first experiences of life on the physical plane. Regardless of how accepting and nurturing a family may be, shame is unavoidable. It is built in to the human condition by the fundamental paradox between soma and psyche at birth. The helplessness of physical and mental immaturity cannot be reconciled with the greatness and majesty of the spirit. Generally, by the time the child begins school, her connection to the sacred mystery is forgotten—programmed out of her by her life experiences or parental disapproval—and in Wordsworth's view, she is left with only "intimations of immortality."

A rare child might be able to recognize this paradox, this inability to access her greatness. I have been told of one little girl who was able to express what she was experiencing. She was a bright little girl, eager to learn, and she was easily frustrated when she was blocked from getting what she wanted. She would throw temper tantrums at home but never in school. One day when she was about seven years old, her mother was at her wit's end trying to keep up with the daughter's demands. The little girl explained that her mother simply had to understand. After all, she said, she was really an old woman in a little girl's body. Needless to say, the mother was taken aback by the truth she sensed in her daughter's statement.

Most children are not as articulate as that seven-year-old girl. Most children do not understand what is happening to them. They experience the conflict between their desire for autonomy and their inability to express their free will, but they cannot endure the tension of the opposition of their inner greatness and their physical limitations. They arrive at the conclusion that they must be at fault. It is their own imperfections, their own flaws, that prevent them from manifesting their beauty and their greatness. They believe they are not good enough to be autonomous. They believe their flaws are not temporary but part of their core character structure. It is a permanent flaw, and they are ashamed of who they are. The connection between their emerging ego and their true spirit personality, their inner higher Self containing the image of God, is severed.

The core of the child's being is no longer filled with mystery and awe but is filled with shame. The child begins to live the illusion that the shameful self is the true core of her being and, in order to endure the pain that the shameful self engenders, dons the mask of *mea culpa*, my fault, "I am to blame." The child feels abandoned. Her young, fragile ego inwardly aligns with this shame, a shame too painful to admit to one's self and too embarrassing to reveal to others. The mea culpa and the shameful self provide the hidden, inner roots for the development of the outward persona, the adaptation the child makes to survive in the physical world. The mea culpa and the shameful self also provide the structure and the nurturance for the inner tyrant.

The dynamics operating at this stage of the child's development are shown in figure 8 on the following page.

The diagram illustrates how the mea culpa and the shameful self block the direct connection between the ego and the authentic Self. The ego, forgetting the existence of the inner higher Self, no longer attempts to connect with that image of God within. The individual, whether child or adult, caught in the illusion that the shameful self is the core of her personality, operates and experiences life from an ego-centered position, where the image of God is outside, not within.

The child dons the mask of the mea culpa as a way of resolving the paradoxical situation between her greatness and her inadequacy. Accepting the blame eases the tension. It eliminates the need to endure the stress engendered by the paradox. The mea culpa becomes her protection, blocking her from looking at her shameful self. As the young

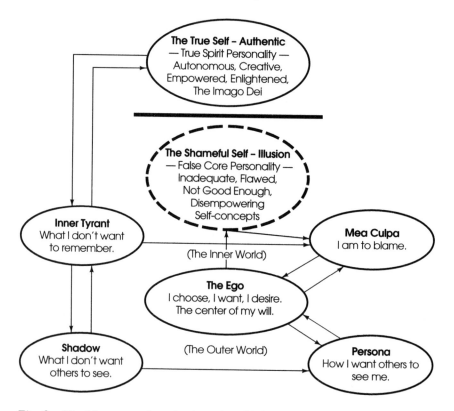

Fig. 8. The false connection: the dynamics of being caught in the illusion that the ego is the center of one's personality

child moves to adapt and survive in the physical world, she drags behind her the guilt and shame of what she believes are her character flaws. While she struggles to develop a persona, her inner tyrant continually reminds her of her flaws and the shame she seeks to hide. This inner dialogue, which she hears from the perspective of the mea culpa, results in a loss of her free will. All of her decisions are predicated on her desire to hide her shame and her guilt. She may believe that she is exercising her free will, but shame and guilt become the hidden determiners, influencing her choices and decisions.

The ego seeks to strengthen the persona, relegating to the shadow any traits, ideas, beliefs, or feelings that do not conform to the image the ego is trying to project. A great deal of energy is directed toward

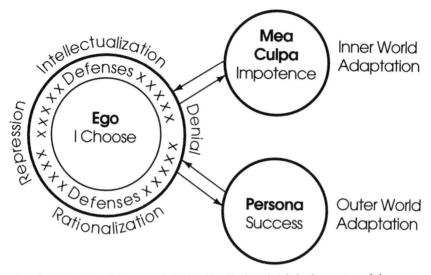

Fig. 9. The defended ego maintaining the illusion that it is the center of the personality

keeping the mask of the persona in place and to keeping the shame hidden from the eyes of others.

At this stage of development it is necessary for the fragile ego to defend itself. As illustrated in figure 9, the ego utilizes repression, intellectualization, denial, rationalization, or other defenses as it connects with the persona and the mea culpa, the two masks worn to assure survival. The persona, as a protection against the outside world that prevents anyone from seeing the naked truth, is an ego defense. The mea culpa is also an ego defense. It protects the ego from seeing itself and from realizing it is not the center of the personality. The mea culpa also protects the ego from remembering, reliving, the bodily experience of shame. The mea culpa, although it is the hidden mask, is the first mask that the ego wears.

The individual's ego struggles to maintain control, struggles to keep the two masks in place. But there is more happening than the ego chooses to acknowledge. Although the ego, forgetting the existence of the inner image of God, no longer feels connected to the Divine, the Self—that is, the inner, authentic, higher Self—does not sever its communication with the ego. As was shown in figure 8, the connection is not a direct one. Communication is maintained by the Self through the inner tyrant and the shadow. The inner tyrant connects to the mea culpa, the shadow impacts the persona, and a continuous link exists between the inner tyrant and the shadow. Although the ego would deny it, it is because of the dark figures of inner tyrant and shadow that future growth and increased consciousness are possible.

Let's take a moment to examine the experience of the father's daughter in the case of the "Rumplestiltskin" maiden—looking at how shame became a part of her being, an integral component of her self-concepts and a hidden determiner of her behavior.

At birth and in early infancy, the baby girl is at one with the Divine; she is infused with the loving energy of the universe in the same way that all children are. As she begins to interact with her environment, she receives love and affirmation from her father. He considers her special and she feels that specialness. At first she does nothing more than be herself, and the love from her father, given just because she is who she is, imbues her with a sense of self-worth. She instinctively moves toward the pleasure she experiences when she is being loved, and she mirrors back to her father her own love for him. At the same time as the baby girl is being affirmed by her father, enjoying the experience of being loved, she is experiencing her own helplessness. He is affirming her, but she is unable to affirm herself. Physically and mentally, she is powerless to manifest her greatness. She cannot exercise her own autonomy, she does not have a sense of personal empowerment. The only power she experiences is the power derived from father through the love and affirmation he gives her. The approval from her father is pronounced. There may or may not be approval from the mother. What is important to the baby daughter and her psychological growth is that she knows she is special in her father's eyes.

As a little child, the father's daughter does not know that her physical limitations will disappear with her maturational development. She is a child with a child's mind and mentally incapable of taking another perspective. She cannot imagine any possibility other than the concrete reality she is experiencing. The truth that she experiences about her self in those moments of early childhood is that she is flawed, she is inadequate, she is powerless. Without her father, she cannot manifest her greatness. Without him, she does not have a sense of self-worth. With him she is somebody, without him she is nobody. Her inadequacies flood her with shame and she turns away from her own inner power, which she cannot manifest. As she turns away, she renounces the possibility of future autonomy. Her movement toward being a father's daughter is reinforced not only by the pleasure she derives from father but also by the relief she feels at distancing herself from the discomfort and pain of her shame.

The outward mask of father's daughter, the persona she wears, reflects her father's values. She can be powerful in the world, getting what she needs to survive, and her persona will hide her shame from other individuals. As the child grows, her adaptation to society generally appears to others to be extremely successful. She has mastered what is expected of her. Her private, inner world, however, is limiting and painful. She has surrendered her connection with her authentic Self. She is ashamed, and her ego defends against the experience of the shameful self, which she believes to be her true core, by donning the mask of mea culpa, "I am at fault."

The two masks are kept in place as the child matures and the dual movement continues. The child reaches for the light, while the roots of shame seek sustenance and support for her outward growth. There comes a time when the father's daughter, as an adult, recognizes the discrepancy between her outer and inner adaptations. It is not uncommon at such a time for a woman to describe herself as a shiny apple with a rotten core.

The longer the father's daughter keeps that persona in place, convincing herself that her outward adaptation is who she truly is, the longer the inner fire of her true spirit remains hidden, covered over with shame. Forgetting who she truly is does not, cannot, extinguish the flame of her authentic Self. The sparks of the Divine, those "clouds of glory," lie waiting to be remembered and recovered.

When the daughter believes her outer adaptation defines who she truly is, she is holding the illusion that her ego is the center of her personality. It is true that the ego is the center of consciousness. It is the organizing principle for choices and decisions. It is the place of "I am," "I want," "I choose," "I will." However, the ego is not the center of her personality. The Self, that image of the Divine within, encompassing both consciousness and the unconscious, is the true center of one's personality. The Self, the authentic center of her being, is the part that has been ignored as the daughter has grown. In truth, the ego and the authentic Self need each other. Without the ego, the authentic Self is a disembodied spirit. Without the authentic Self, the individual ego is a spiritless two-legged, not a human being. It is in the relationship between the authentic Self and the ego that spirit becomes substance and substance returns to spirit.

Jung has said that when the individual becomes aware that the ego is not the center of one's personality, a shift occurs that is akin to the earth recognizing that the sun, not the earth, is the center of the solar system.

The little girl grows into an adult, and the memory of greatness fades into forgetfulness. The two masks are firmly in place: the persona for adaptation to the outer world, the mea culpa for adapting to the inner world. The task of remembering, of reconciling the ego with the authentic Self, requires that both masks be removed, that both masks be seen and honored for what they are, namely, the defenses of a small child that were necessary for survival.

It is never too late to begin remembering. The life experiences that engender shame are like rocks or stones placed on an emerging plant. The plant grows around the blocks, continually moving toward the light. Later, when the stone is removed, the bend in the plant remains. In the same way, one's story, one's own history, remains a fact in one's life. However, the new growth in the plant and the new growth in an individual is straight and true.

The moment of removing the stone or pushing it aside is the moment of change, the moment when the woman chooses, with free will, to regain her autonomy. In "Rumplestiltskin," the maiden/queen is a father's daughter caught in the web spun between the mea culpa and the shameful self. She is encouraged by the dwarf to remain in the web. But in truth, it is the demanding dwarf who finally pushes her to the point where she begins to reclaim her autonomy. She does this by discarding the perspective of the mea culpa and addressing her inner tyrant directly. The moment she addresses her inner tyrant, she begins the process of reconnecting with the Self.

The fairy tale does not tell us what happens next to the queen. However, the tale does provide a clue as to what her future process might involve. We are told that the queen mourns the potential loss of her baby. The hint in the fairy tale is that emotions are the key. That hint suggests that it is through the emotions that today's father's daughters will glimpse the possibilities that lie in their future. They may also discover what has prevented them from changing the myth that has limited their experience of life. It may be that other individuals will find emotions a key for them as well.

Note that Erik Erikson's scheme of psychosocial stages posits that the dichotomy of autonomy versus shame and doubt occurs at the toddler stage, from ages one to three years. Erikson's eight life stages concern the ego's development in adjusting to the physical world—in other words, the individual's psychosocial adaptation. I agree with the dichotomy of autonomy versus shame, but in the conceptualization I am offering, the shame does not disappear with the toddler's adaptation to societal expectations, e.g., becoming toilet trained. The shame, in my view, is a result of not being able to access one's spiritual glory. Even though the child is adjusting to societal expectations, she knows in her heart of hearts that she is not autonomous, not truly independent. A part of her knows that she should be independent. The shame she experiences, hidden from view because it is too painful to admit, exerts a powerful influence over her behavior.

Chapter Seven
Emotions as Teachers

In "Rumplestiltskin," at the moment when the queen realizes that the cost of continuing in her role of father's daughter is more than she can afford, that it is no less than the total surrender of all future life for herself, she mourns, grief-stricken. The reality of what she has been doing to herself has slapped her in the face. No longer can she distort reality. She has been living a lie and she knows it. She is caught, psychologically, in a life-and-death conflict. Until this moment, she believed that being a handmaiden to the lord — whether the lord was father, husband, or culture — was her destiny, her truth, her completeness. She thought that she would have a full life because she was being the person she believed she was born to be. But now she sees her reality, her life, as it truly is. She has been living an illusion. Her life as a father's daughter was a role assigned to her, a role she accepted and now sees as too costly to maintain. And she grieves.

In this interaction, the fairy tale points out a psychic truth. Intellectual, mental understanding of a conflict is not enough by itself. The abstraction of intellectual understanding must be integrated and assimilated in the body through the emotions. Then and only then is one's own truth known. Illusions are burned away by the fire of the emotions. In the fairy tale, the queen's intellectual understanding is accompanied by her emotions — her grieving — and through her grief, she is incarnating her truth. The fairy tale does not go into details of the process, but, according to Jung, increased consciousness follows the road illuminated by the emotions. Jung wrote:

> The stirring up of a conflict is a Luciferian virtue in the true sense of the word. Conflict engenders fire, the fire of affects and emotions, and like every other fire it has two aspects, that of combustion and

that of creating light. On the one hand, emotion is the alchemical fire whose warmth brings everything into existence and whose heat burns all superfluities to ashes (*omnes superfluitates comburit*). But on the other hand, emotion is the moment when steel meets flint and a spark is struck forth, for emotion is the chief source of consciousness. There is no change from darkness to light or from inertia to movement without emotion. (Jung 1954, par. 179)

Let us back up for a moment and examine the psychological dynamics of a father's daughter before she experiences a conflict with her role. This would be something like the way the maiden/queen in "Rumplestiltskin" functions before naming the dwarf.

In figure 10 on the following page, which is extracted from figure 8 in the previous chapter, the maiden's defended ego is shown wearing two masks, the persona and the mea culpa. The energy of the maiden/queen, as she lives her life as a father's daughter, is directed toward those two masks. This is all she chooses to see or acknowledge. A large percentage of her energy is directed toward the outer world, toward her persona, toward fulfilling the role of father's daughter, which she does well and which she believes defines who she truly is. She diminishes or ignores any part of her personality that does not conform to the expectations associated with the role her father has assigned her. In other words, she wants nothing to do with her shadow. She turns her back on the inferior aspects of her personality—those negative ideas, concepts, traits, and behaviors that conflict with how she wishes to be seen. She has also relegated to her shadow all the emotions she has chosen not to experience, those emotions she had cut off from consciousness in her first transaction with the dwarf.

The remainder of the maiden/queen's energy—that is, the energy under her conscious ego control—is directed toward keeping the inner mask of the mea culpa in place. In her heart of hearts, she believes that when she is on her own, she is impotent. Her body contains memory traces of the shame she experienced in infancy and early childhood from her lack of autonomy. She does not want to remember or reexperience the shame or the tension associated with her helplessness. By keeping her inner mask of mea culpa in place, she forms a wall, a boundary, between her ego and what she believes is the bottomless pit of her shameful self. The inner mask of the mea culpa keeps the shame at bay, and both the mea culpa and the shameful self block any awareness of her inner greatness. She can handle the limitations imposed by the mea

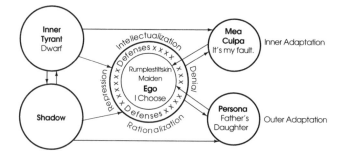

Fig. 10. How her father's daughter functions before naming the dwarf

culpa; she sees as normal the doubts she experiences about herself and her abilities. She cannot handle the feeling of shame. The mea culpa is her mental perspective. It is her belief that she is not autonomous, that she cannot stand alone. This is an inner dynamic that she does not show to the outer world. The mea culpa reinforces for her the necessity of adapting to the role of father's daughter. It points out to her that it is only through being a father's daughter that she receives any affirmation. The mea culpa is the first mask that the father's daughter wears; in fact, it is the first mask that anyone wears. The father's daughter dons the mea culpa even before assuming her persona.

The mea culpa is as critical to the development of the ego as the persona is. The mea culpa allows the individual to separate from the containment of the inner self. It is a necessary step in the path toward consciousness. As her ego turns away from the inner higher Self, believing that the core of her personality is a shameful abyss, the father's daughter begins to see the image of the Divine as outside of herself. She is convinced that she is alone. She alone determines what she must do. Her ego, she believes, is the center of her total personality.

As figure 10 shows, in the ego-centered personality – that is, in an individual who has no awareness of the Divine within – the energy moves in a loop between the mea culpa and the persona, passing always through the ego. It is the ego that focuses attention on one or the other. The two masks are interdependent. A change in the mea culpa would mean a change in the persona, and vice versa. No direct connection exists between the mea culpa and the persona; all energy passes through the defended ego, reinforcing its belief that it is the center of the personality.

The ego of the father's daughter who has not yet named the dwarf directs no energy toward incorporating the contents of the shadow or questioning the voice of the inner tyrant. Whatever resides in the shadow and whatever is spoken by the inner tyrant are matters to be shunned or ignored. Although the individual, with her ego, may choose to ignore the shadow and the inner tyrant, these two forces are not dormant. The shadow continually impacts the persona, deepening its imperfections, while the inner tyrant constantly reminds the mea culpa of its inadequacies and the shame lurking just beyond that inner mask.

To clarify what I am theorizing, let me refer back to an example I gave earlier. In chapter four, I discussed the challenge I faced as I struggled to complete my training as a Jungian analyst. I wrote of how I discovered a dwarf to be my inner tyrant. Prior to recognizing this tyrant, I had been beset by doubts. I wondered if I could complete my task. I questioned if I was being foolish or even ridiculous in attempting to do what I wanted to do. I thought, "Maybe it really is too much." There were no guarantees and I wanted a guarantee. I did not want to be embarrassed by failing. The inner tyrant, I discovered as I listened closely, was suggesting to my mea culpa that I was going to be shamed. Until I stopped and listened carefully to what was being said, my mea culpa—the doubting, self-limiting part of myself—took the messages from that inner tyrant as truth. The mea culpa was my mind-set that I was at fault for not being able to be the person I wanted to be. It was my fault, my limitations, that stood in the way.

In the conceptualization of the psyche that I am offering here, the shadow and the inner tyrant occasionally break through the ego's defenses and impact the ego directly. The shadow and the inner tyrant are connected to one another. In fact, there is a perpetual connection, for the shadow and the inner tyrant are both fed by their link to the inner higher Self. In my example, the shadow reinforced the inner tyrant because I did not want to be wrong or make a mistake. In my persona, I struggled for perfection.

In "Rumplestiltskin," it is at the point of grieving that the maiden/queen opens her defended ego to her shadow and begins the painful task of assimilating what she has repressed. Figure 11 on the following page depicts the psychological dynamics that are at work as she begins the process of remembering what she has paid to be a father's daughter and allows herself to experience her loss of autonomy.

As the maiden/queen chooses to face her shadow, she admits into consciousness what previously she had excluded from her persona. In

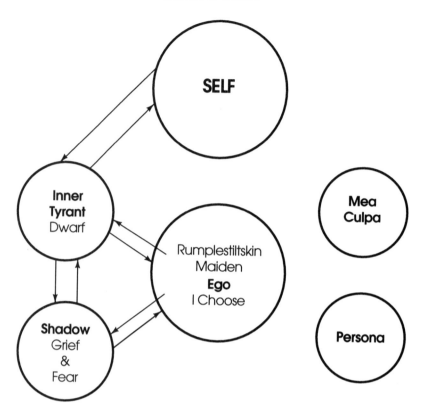

Fig. 11. The Rumplestiltskin maiden at the point of remembering the cost and beginning to address the inner tyrant

admitting these shadow contents, she is allowing her fears and inferiori-ties to enter into the central place of her determining ego.

The process of willingly integrating her shadow, suffering the truth of what she has wrought, connects the maiden/queen in a new way to her inner tyrant, the dwarf. It is after her grieving that, unexpectedly, the dwarf offers her a way out of her predicament. In figure 11, the arrows depict the new flow of energy between the ego and the shadow and between the ego and the inner tyrant, which results in an opening, a broadening, an increase in ego consciousness. The mea culpa and the persona are still present, but no longer are they the sole recipients of the ego's attention. The maiden/queen's attention is now turned to her shadow and she experiences grief.

The repressed contents of the shadow always have an emotional component, as Jung has noted. In his essay on the shadow, Jung wrote: "A closer examination of the dark characteristics—that is, the inferiorities constituting the shadow—reveals that they have an *emotional* nature" (1951, par. 15). When Jung wrote that statement, he was describing the characteristics of the shadow as it occurred in all human beings, not just women, and certainly not just father's daughters. Thus one could ask, what are the emotions that are connected to shadow contents? Or, are all emotions shadowy?

One of the hallmarks of being human is having emotions, having the ability to laugh and to cry. Laughing when we are joyous and crying when we are sad are a significant part of what differentiates us from the animal kingdom. They are part of our authenticity, our autonomy. But emotions, besides defining our humanity, can also be hindrances to the human spirit. Fear, anger, depression, frustration, hysteria, anxiety, jealousy, envy, rage—not to mention guilt and shame—all limit our potential and affect our functioning. We can be caught by these emotions and lose our autonomy. For example, if we are caught in revenge—or even in a milder form of revenge, the desire to get even—we are reacting with a kind of knee-jerk response. We are not autonomous, we are not exercising our free will. When the emotions happen to us, taking us over, they and the repressed shadow qualities determine how we are behaving—we do not.

As I have worked with emotions, both in my own process and those of my analysands, I have found repeated confirmation of Jung's assertion that emotions are connected with our imperfections. Those aspects of our personalities that are out of alignment with our persona are emotionally charged. When I reflected on the full range of emotions, including those listed above, without any preconceived ideas, a new configuration of emotions emerged, revealing what I now believe are the fundamental emotions. In the outer world, the fundamental emotion is fear. In the inner world, the fundamental emotion is shame. On these two emotions all others rest. I know there are other ways of looking at emotions. One of the most helpful for me has come from the Twisted Hair tradition that I study. This tradition, incorporating teachings from many Native American tribes, classifies all emotions that humans experience in their day-to-day relationships into four major categories: fear, depression, anger, and stress, with stress including both hysteria and anxiety. These are general categories, including other emotions within them. For example, anger includes a continuum of emotions from frustration to rage. But regardless of the groupings, it is my contention that fear is the basic emotion, the common affect underlying all our interactions and relationships in the physical world.

In my view, depression, anger, and stress (and all the emotions contained within those categories) are all secondary characteristics of fear. For example, with depression there is an underlying fear that one is powerless, and this connects to a fear of claiming and exercising one's own power. There is also a fear of being responsible for one's own choices. With anger, one insists on having one's own way, and there is a fear of not being in control, of not being right, of confronting the unknown.

With stress, whether hysteria or anxiety, one is continually comparing oneself to others. There is a feeling of inadequacy, and the individual is constantly trying to conform to someone else's way of being or doing. One is always looking to others for affirmation. There is a fear of being alone and an underlying fear of not being good enough in oneself.

From my perspective, regardless of which emotion is first experienced by the ego as it engages the shadow, eventually and inevitably, the ego must address and assimilate fear.

As I have said, fear is the basic emotion of one's external, objective relationships and shame is the underlying emotion in our inner subjective experience. Fear and shame are not unrelated; they connect with each other. We are ashamed of being fearful and fearful of experiencing shame. The inner world of shame includes the emotion of guilt. Also included are embarrassment and humiliation. Guilt arises when rules are broken. The rules—which an individual has been taught by family, culture, peer group, and so on—concern a collectively established morality. They are like taboos. Guilt, as well as fear, bridges the outer and inner worlds of one's experience. Embarrassment and humiliation are connected to one's inadequacies, to one's failings, whether real or imagined. They generally are experienced more acutely when another person is present to witness one's shortcomings.

Originally I thought that in the process of remembering who one truly is, the ego would move first to assimilate the inferior aspects of the shadow. Now I am not so certain. What the ego is to address, where it is to begin the process of individuation, is always orchestrated by the events of one's life and one's own inner higher self. It could be that time and circumstances fall into place in such a way that the individual chooses to begin the process of remembering by addressing the inner tyrant. What I do know with certainty is that the inner tyrant and the emotional contents of the shadow are connected. When the individual begins working on the inner tyrant, she will be led automatically to the shadow, and vice versa. The emotions are the common thread between the two.

I have developed a process for working with the emotions that is based upon Jungian theory. I call the process emotional clearing, and have found it helpful to individuals who choose to move toward increased consciousness. It is a process that may be used by anyone, not only those who are in formal Jungian psychoanalysis. When I instruct analysands in this process, I remind them that they are their own best teachers and that they are in control. They will be setting the parameters of the experience. The particular emotion they will be addressing comes out of their own individuation process. Generally, the analysands do not engage in this process during the analytic session. There are exceptions to this, which I will address later in this chapter.

Using emotions as a red thread to guide one in untangling the repetitive patterns of self-defeating behaviors is an idea that is not foreign to Jungian psychology. In his essay, "The Transcendent Function" (1958), Jung touches on various methods an individual could employ when addressing the unconscious. He saw the emotions as the starting place for an individual attempting to retrieve from the unconscious, material and energy that belonged in consciousness. The material that would be retrieved was material needed to correct a one-sided position. For example, it could be like the maiden/queen in "Rumplestiltskin" attempting to correct the one-sidedness of her mind-set as a father's daughter. Jung was describing a technique he called *active imagination* when he wrote, in that essay: "In order, therefore, to gain possession of the energy that is in the wrong place, [s]he must make the emotional state the basis or starting point of the procedure" (ibid., par. 167). Later in the same article he wrote: "The purpose . . . is to discover the feeling-toned contents, for in these cases we are always dealing with situations where the one-sidedness of consciousness meets with the resistance of the instinctual sphere" (ibid., par. 178).

Jung also wrote that it was important in the process that "the position of the ego be maintained as being of equal value to the counterposition of the unconscious and vice-versa" (ibid., par. 183). This statement, I believe, describes the crucial factor in determining whether or not an individual can engage the process of emotional clearing by herself or not. If she is able to maintain an ego position that invites the unconscious, whether shadow contents or inner tyrant, to participate in a partnership—a dance, if you will—then she is capable of engaging this process by herself. If, however, she has been so traumatized that she has difficulty in moving out of the victim stance, then the participation of the analyst is necessary to buttress her ego. This occurs in cases of multiple personality disorder or similarly charged traumatic complexes.

The process of emotional clearing is not one of just being emotional or emoting for emotion's sake, but of embodying and retrieving into consciousness what was too painful to experience at an earlier time. The process is initiated when the individual analysand recognizes that a particular emotion is interfering in her life.

I caution analysands, when they begin their emotional clearing, not to discuss the process with anyone else, but to hold the tension that the process generates until our next session. Talking with others about what one is experiencing delays or even prevents the desired change, the transformation, from occurring. It is the same as when a seed is planted. It needs the protection of darkness in order to sprout. Unearthing the seed to examine what is happening brings light too soon to the process and may delay or even prevent the tender roots from taking form.

Alchemically, containing the tension keeps the retort closed, allowing something new to be created when the inferior, base materials are transformed by the heat. Holding the tension is identical to what occurs in formal Jungian analysis. In discussing the need to hold the tension, a colleague of mine, Tom Lavin, referred to the alchemical metaphor of finding the philosopher's stone in the dung heap. Keeping the lid on the pot containing the dung causes the pot to boil faster than if you take the lid off to see how it is doing. The pot may eventually come to a boil with the lid off, but there are no guarantees. The choice is up to the individual as to whether or not the tension will be held. With that introduction and caution, I give the following guidelines for using emotions as teachers.

The Process of Clearing the Emotions

1. First of all, find a space and a time where you can be safe and alone.

2. Make the space your sacred space. I do this by incorporating what I have learned from a variety of traditions. You may do this in any way that you wish. For example, you may wish to have objects that are sacred to you arranged on an altar. I arrange four small bowls in the four cardinal directions, form-

ing a circle around me. In the south, I place a bowl of water, in the west, a bowl of earth, in the north, I place incense in the bowl, and in the east bowl, I place a candle.

3. Determine how long you choose to be actively sitting with this emotion. Will it be ten minutes, twenty minutes, or two minutes? You decide how long and then set an alarm clock or a timer for the length of time you have chosen. Having set an alarm, you will not be distracted by thinking about the time. You will not have to wonder: "How much longer do I have to be sitting here?"

4. Sit up. This process is not to be done lying down. You can sit on the floor, you can sit on a chair, but it is important that you are upright.

5. At this point you pray. I generally sit cross-legged within the circle with my hands, palms up, resting on my knees. I take this position, copied from the Islamic tradition, as a way of stating that I will receive whatever is revealed to me. I am surrendering, by choice, the need to be in control of what comes up. You may call in whatever higher power you choose. Following the Twisted Hair tradition, I then call in all of my ancestors who have loved me since always. Call in those relatives, those ancestors of yours, whom you know loved you dearly who are no longer alive.

6. Then remember the emotion. With your imagination, put yourself back into the situation where you last experienced the emotion.

7. Feel the emotion in your body.

8. Pay attention to what is happening. Be an observer. Do not intellectualize, do not wonder what is going to happen or why this is happening. Stay alert and in the moment.

9. Continue until the alarm goes off. If your mind wanders, focus back into the moment, back into the situation where you are experiencing the emotion. You are engaging in an act of split

attention. You are in your body and at the same time, you are observing what is happening to your body.

10. When the alarm goes off, journal about what you have experienced. You may receive an image, you may retrieve a memory, you may hear a voice speaking in your head. Whatever you experienced, write it in your journal with no judgments, comments, elaborations, or speculations.

11. Thank the higher power, or powers, and the ancestors that you have called in for being present and for witnessing your ceremony.

12. Before you leave your sacred space, you may want to determine when you next will actively sit with your emotions. If so, write the date and the time you have decided upon in your journal.

Usually many sittings are required to integrate the emotional shadow contents. It could take several months to discover all the ramifications of one particular emotion, all the relationships and behaviors that have been controlled from the shadows by that one particular emotion.

After the session of actively engaging the emotion is over, you may examine and analyze your journal entry. This is the time when the intellect is utilized to understand the contents—symbols, memories, whatever—that have been retrieved. At this time, it is the woman, not the child, who determines the meaning of the past events. It is the woman, with her adult perspective, who decides what is to be done. This correlates with the point in "Rumplestiltskin" where the queen begins to act independently, summoning the messenger to scour the countryside. It is as Jung has said: the emotions have provided the energy to move from inertia to action.

It is possible in this process of clearing the emotions that an early traumatic experience will be remembered and recognized as the core of the problem. This is unusual. It is more likely that no significant, single trauma will be remembered but rather an accumulation of emotional experiences throughout one's lifetime. Individually, each of these remembered events are not terribly significant, but together they, like the relentless drop-by-drop method of the Chinese water torture, cause excruciating pain. Remembering the events and integrating the emotions associated with them will decrease the compulsion to repeat the old patterns, which have reinforced one's lack of autonomy.

In working through the emotional contents of the shadow and integrating what were formerly viewed as inferior aspects of one's personality, the father's daughter—or anyone for that matter—will no longer be ruled by the past, by childhood beliefs and assumptions. In the shamanic tradition of the Twisted Hairs, the first major task in becoming a woman or man of power is called erasing one's personal history. Clearing the emotions does erase from one's personal history the underlying cause of one's self-defeating behaviors—the feeling that one lacks autonomy. Being free of childish attitudes and behaviors allows one to move into a position where, as a contemporary Twisted Hair, Swift Deer, has said: "The future determines the present, the past only predicates the form."

The process, as Jung has said, is one of circumambulation, of withdrawing one ember at a time from the emotional fire. Doing it at one's own pace, staying in charge of the parameters of the process—determining when, where, and for how long—prevents one from getting burned or consumed by the fire.

Engaging the dance with one's higher power through clearing one's emotions demands that one assume authority for oneself. It demands and requires that one choose when and how to begin. The individual ego initiates the process but both the ego and the inner higher Self collaborate on how long and how intense the dance will be.

In all of my work, I have found that the Self, one's inner higher Self, is never wrong in what it presents to the ego as the current issue needing to be addressed. When I have used my intellect, thinking I knew what an individual should be addressing in analysis, I have been wrong many times. I now know that I am a witness to the process, a witness to the fire—a container of sorts—holding mirrors for the analysand to look into. I am a reflecting, interacting energy, observing what the analysand's higher Self presents through dreams, emotions, and life circumstances. I also know that these are teachings for me, as well.

Symbols occur not only in the dream state of an analysand but in our day-to-day activities. Those highly charged moments in our everyday relationships are as revealing and important to our personal growth as the numinous symbols in our dreams that wake us from our slumbers. Either can become the starting point for increased awareness of who we truly are.

Chapter Eight

The Mythic Pattern
on the World Stage

Looking at father's daughters from the perspective of their inner tyrants, their shadowy unlived sides, and their emotional realities reveals
much about the psychology of these women. However, there is another
perspective that can be taken, which provides clues to what the future
holds for father's daughters. This is the perspective provided when we
examine father's daughters against the backdrop of mythic patterns on
the world stage. It is a perspective that affords us a developmental
cosmic view and that may have applications even for women who are
not father's daughters as well as for men.

No one lives in a vacuum. We are all interrelated, and what happens
to one individual affects another. Further, a connection exists between
what happens within us, in our psyches, and what happens outside of
us, in our relationships. The outer world mirrors our inner world and
vice versa. The mythic patterns in the macrocosm of the outer world—
whether our family, our culture, or the world stage—reflect the myths
we hold in the microcosmic world, containing our inner, private beliefs
and values. The relationship is reciprocal so that, although our outer
world is a mirror of our inner world, the outer world, the culture in
which we live, helps shape the myths we hold as truths. The connection
between the inner and outer worlds is such that if a change occurs in
one domain, say within an individual's psyche, it will cause a shift, a
change, to occur in the other domain, within one's family for example.
When an individual changes—that is, when one person increases in
consciousness or adopts new beliefs—a shift occurs on the world stage,
even though it may be as infinitesimal as a grain of sand. All major
changes on the world stage are the result of individuals changing, one by
one.

The patriarchal era in which we are living is said to have existed for five thousand years and to have been preceded by a matriarchal era of 25,000 years. Father's daughters, as we have defined them, are women who seek their fathers' approval and uphold their fathers' values in supporting the patriarchal culture. Father's daughters are a product, a phenomenon, of the patriarchal era. We may well ask what called forth the emergence of father's daughters? Where did the shift occur on the world stage to make being a father's daughter more appealing to little girls than being a mother's daughter? What are the differences between the matriarchal and patriarchal eras? Let's take a moment to gain a panoramic view of the world stage, gleaning what we can about the movement from the past into the present as it relates to father's daughters. Then perhaps we can intuit future possibilities for these women.

In the matriarchal era, one's lineage was established by one's maternal bloodline. The mystery of birth and the mysteries of blood – the monthly bleeding of menstruation and the lactation of nursing mothers – were the powerful symbols giving women supremacy in the matriarchal era (Neumann 1974). Matriarchy was rule by the mother, and the most heinous crime one could commit was murdering one's mother. The law of the matriarchy, the law of the blood, was protected by the Furies, who avenged any wrongs against the mother. The relentless Furies were so feared that even Zeus, head of the Olympic gods and goddesses, would not tangle with them. The power and fearsomeness of the Furies is remembered even today with statements like "Hell hath no fury like a woman scorned."

While it was important in the matriarchal era to know one's mother, it was not important to know one's father. In, fact, the male role in procreation was not understood. So the dynamic of young girls adopting the values of their fathers and seeking their fathers' approval would have been highly unlikely. Fathers did not have power, mothers did.

We can only speculate about what happened as the majority of the world switched from matriarchal to patriarchal societies, but myth and art provide hints about the dynamics operating at that time of transition. The view from the world stage will show the reversal in the roles of women, who moved from being dominant in the matriarchal world to being subordinate in the patriarchal one.

Scholars hypothesize that the organization and structure of the matriarchal societies were fundamentally different from those of patriarchy. Matriarchal societies were thought to be built upon a partnership model while patriarchal societies are seen as based on a hierarchical, dominator model (Eisler 1986). This hypothesis may be accurate in describing differences in social structures, but it certainly is not true in describing the differences between the religions of the two eras.

In matriarchal cultures, the mother goddess was supreme. There was no partnership. The triune mother goddess of maiden, matron, and crone did not have a father god as her equal. Her consort in his most developed form was a son-lover. In certain cultures, her son-lover was sacrificed annually to assure the fertility of the land (Graves 1948; Fraser 1922). The mother goddess was jealous of her power and slapped down those who opposed her (Meador 1987); she was no more willing to share her power than any of the patriarchal father gods who followed her were willing to share theirs. The Christian trinity of Father, Son, and Holy Ghost, for example, admits the feminine into the inner circle of power only as a virgin who is the handmaiden of the Lord. This patriarchal arrangement of the masculine and feminine is the exact opposite of the imbalance that occurred in the matriarchal era with the feminine trinity.

An examination of the art of the past does reveal many differences between matriarchal and patriarchal cultures. None is more significant than the different treatments accorded sexuality and the body. In the matriarchal world, the body and sexuality were honored and enjoyed. Pictures and statues from the matriarchal era depict goddesses and women who are naked or whose breasts are bared and whose bodies are entwined by snakes. The art from that era also reveals male nudity, with masculine genitalia openly displayed.

Women, under the matriarchy, were free to enjoy their sexuality with whomever they chose. No wonder it was not important to know who one's father was; it might have been impossible to tell. This is possibly another reason why the dynamics of father's daughters would have been unknown during the height of the matriarchal era. It was mother's law and mother's values that were honored in the matriarchy. Young girls, born in the image of the goddess, probably relished that fact. It does not take much imagination to envision these young girls, and perhaps all women, beginning each morning with a prayer expressing their gratitude to the goddess for making them female and not male.

As the world pendulum swung, moving from matriarchal supremacy to patriarchal ascendancy, women were separated from their right to free sexual expression. No longer was matricide the unforgivable crime. No longer was the bloodline of the mother the all-important factor in one's identity. Now the role of the male in procreation not only was acknowledged, it was becoming the decisive factor in one's heritage.

The dynamics between feminine and masculine energies were reversing. In the inevitable action that Jung named *enantiodromia*, during which that which is repressed emerges into consciousness, the arc of the pendulum peaked and women's sexuality fell under male dominance.

This moment of transition – when matriarchy was replaced by patriarchy and women lost their sexual independence – is told in the mythical story of Adam and Eve and the serpent in the Garden of Eden. This biblical story relates that after Eve ate of the fruit of the tree of knowledge – after she ingested the apple that would allow her, and Adam, to know good and evil – Yahweh, the patriarchal father god, exiled Eve and Adam from Paradise. Before exiling them, however, Yahweh put enmity between Eve and the snake. He did not put enmity between Adam and the snake nor between Adam and Eve. He only put his judgment, his curse, between the woman and the snake. And in a later passage in Genesis, women are told they will find their sexual satisfaction in and through their husbands. What does this mean symbolically?

In the matriarchal tradition, the snake symbolized the life-force energy and the life-force energy was sexual energy. Entwined around goddess figurines, the snake depicted a woman at one with her sexuality and with her body (Neumann 1974, p. 83). It was not only the fecundity of women that the snake represented but orgiastic, sexual delight (Pagels 1982, 1992). Sexuality, for the Great Mother, was divine, and the snake represented that aspect of divinity (Meador 1992, pp. 92–103).

In the world of animals, it is the snake who is the closest to the earth. It crawls on its belly on earth, on matter, on mother. Because of its shape, it has a phallic connotation and, for the Great Mother Goddess, the snake represented the conceptive, masculine part of the birth process. As kundalini in Tantric traditions, the snake represents sexual, life-force energy, whether it is in relationship with women or with men. The snake and sexuality are inseparable. When Yahweh put enmity between Eve and the snake, it meant that in the patriarchal world, woman and her sexuality – her instinctive, ecstatic, orgiastic energy – would be separated. The two would become enemies. Women would continue to birth children, but sexual pleasure would be denied. The birth of a child would now be associated with pain. No longer would it be as it was in the past, when giving birth was experienced as a giant orgasm. No longer would a woman value menstruation, the time of her peak sexual arousal, the time when she could enjoy sexual intercourse without conceiving a child (Shuttle and Redgrove 1978, pp. 87–94). A

73

woman's menstrual blood now became a symbol of her uncleanliness. She was cursed. The beauty and majesty of the woman's ecstatic sexuality were reduced to pleasureless, if not painful, procreation. The expulsion from the garden tells of the pain that women were to suffer as the matriarchal era ended and the patriarchy began.

Mythical stories from other cultures, such as ancient Greece, parallel the Bible's myths in telling how women's sexual freedom was restricted as part of their subjugation in male-dominated cultures. An examination of particular Greek myths may help illuminate that transitional time by providing a different perspective from the one given by the Biblical stories. With the Greek myths, we can glimpse a different culture on the world stage as it moved toward embracing the father gods.

Among the pantheon of Greek gods and goddesses, the archetypal father's daughter was Athena. She was born from the head of her father, Zeus, wearing golden armor so bright it rivaled the sun (Graves 1977, 9.b). The myth states that as she emerged from Zeus's head, being freed only because she gave him a raging headache, she removed her armor and laid it down. Thereafter, if she ever had need of a shield or a helmet, she borrowed them. In what follows, in retelling the myths of Athena, I will be offering interpretations that are mine and frequently differ from the interpretations offered by others (Loomis 1982).

Athena was within her father, Zeus, the myth relates, because Zeus feared the potential of his pregnant wife, a powerful elemental goddess. He tricked her into becoming a fly and then swallowed her to contain her (Graves 1977, 9b; Downing 1981, p. 119). In symbolic language, this myth tells of the devouring, the swallowing up, of the matriarchal cultures by the patriarchy. However, the power of the matriarchy does not disappear. It lies within the patriarchy, hidden in the shadows. Athena, conceived by the union of the new, clever patriarchy and the overconfident, unconscious matriarchy, grows into adulthood encapsulated in her father. She symbolizes how the matriarchy's unlimited powers were reshaped, confined, by the boundaries and limit-setting imposed by the patriarchy. This myth depicts how the matriarchy and the matriarchal energies were forced into reflecting upon themselves. Athena's nature, her lineage, is the matriarchy; her nurture, her training, is the patriarchy. When, at her birth, Athena lays down the golden armor that symbolizes patriarchal power and might, she once again reveals her feminine and matriarchal allegiance. But it is the matriarchy in transition, the matriarchy confronted by the patriarchy, that she represents.

She is the father's daughter, and it is she along with Zeus and Apollo who are the most revered by the Greeks. The matriarchy did not disappear from the rings of power. It was assuming a new form.

This father's daughter, Athena, was known as the goddess of wisdom. Some have called her the goddess of war, but that is inaccurate. The god of war was Mars—impulsive, overreactive, unthinking. Athena always used her head. She was not afraid to fight, but she fought with wisdom; the result was that she never lost a battle. In fact, she fought twice with her brother Mars and defeated him both times (Graves 1977, 19b). Athena was the mistress of proper timing. She is the embodiment of what we would call the observing ego, and it is her use of her intellect—her wisdom and her reflective capacities—that are relevant to this examination of the patterns on the world stage, particularly the patterns involving the matriarchy and sexuality.

Athena combined intellect with instinctive sexuality. Some writers have called her a traitor to the matriarchy (Bolen 1984) because some of her actions limited the unbridled powers of mother law. These charges of being a traitor are leveled at Athena primarily because of her actions at the trial of Orestes, but they could also be leveled at her for her treatment of Medusa.

The Greek myths tell us that Orestes was on trial for matricide (Graves 1977, 114.n; Grene and Lattimore 1959, p. 161). He had murdered his mother to avenge the death of his father. His mother, with the aid of her paramour, had killed his father because the father had broken the law of the blood by sacrificing one of their children. Athena presided at the trial of Orestes, where the Furies were demanding Orestes' death. The Furies maintained that the mother's killing of her husband was not a serious crime because they were not blood relatives, but Orestes' murder of his mother was unforgivable. He had broken the law of the blood. At this time in history, the role of the male in procreation was beginning to be recognized, although there was still no understanding of the sperm and the ovum. What was gaining acceptance was a belief that the semen carried a homunculus, a microscopic person, that grew to infant size within the womb of the woman. This belief denied that a woman had any blood connection with the child born from her womb. It was this argument that was presented as Orestes' defense. When the ballots were counted, there was a tie, which ordinarily would have automatically condemned Orestes. But Athena cast the deciding vote, a vote for his acquittal. It was a deliberate choice. She did not have to vote, but she chose to act.

Up until this point in history matriarchal law, enforced by the Furies, was absolute. The only law was the law of the blood. No mitigating circumstances were allowed or considered in rendering judicial decrees involving transgressions of the blood. Athena broke the pattern. She weighed and evaluated the mitigating circumstances. Also, prior to casting her vote, Athena addressed the Furies; she did not renounce them. She spoke with them, reasoning with them, and proposed to build an altar for them where they can be honored (Hillman 1980, p. 18). The Furies never had an altar before this time, nor had they been honored, only feared. Athena convinced them with words and logic to accept a place in this new order. It was only after the Furies agreed to accept her offer that Athena, remaining loyal to the powers of the matriarchy, cast her vote.

Athena's behavior at the trial of Orestes symbolically marks a transition in psychological development. Human consciousness moved from a childish position of moral absolutism to a position capable of considering intent and mitigating circumstances in establishing justice and morality. Athena represents the father's daughter who continues to honor the matriarchy but incorporates wisdom in her decisions. She is not blind.

The necessity for wisdom as the patterns on the world stage were changing is also revealed in Athena's treatment of Medusa. Here the mythic focus is on Athena's relationship to sexuality. Originally, Medusa was a goddess, and as a goddess she enjoyed her sexuality and engaged in sexual activities instinctively wherever and whenever she chose. Her unrestrained sexuality resulted in her having sexual intercourse in front of an altar dedicated to Athena. Athena, as the goddess of wisdom, was outraged, feeling her altar had been defiled by Medusa's unthinking behavior (Graves 1977, 33b). Medusa, as one of the old goddesses, acted on every impulse. She did not pause to reflect, she did not think before she acted. Athena retaliated by changing Medusa into a gorgon with a head full of writhing snakes, symbolizing her unbridled sexuality. The raw power of sexuality, however, could not be denied. Anyone gazing at Medusa and her head full of snakes would be turned to stone — that is, they would be caught, immobilized, by the power of instinctual sexuality.

Through Athena's assistance and planning, Medusa finally was decapitated. This came about when Athena gave Perseus a shield to use as a mirror (Graves 1977, 73f). By looking at Medusa in reflection, Perseus could guide his sword and not be turned to stone. The use of the shield as a mirror highlights the necessity of reflection when dealing with instinctual energies. The beheading of Medusa signaled the final depotentiation of sexuality as the primary function of the Divine. Instinct and the body, which had encompassed the Divine essence in the matriarchal era, were no longer able to contain the broader scope of the divinity. Logos had to be incorporated into Eros.

In the myth, Athena eventually wears Medusa's head on her aegis, the leather protection she wears in front of her as a shield, and thus she signals her continued connection to her sexuality (Graves 1977, 33b). But no longer is sexuality supreme; it has been tempered with wisdom.

On the world stage, the matriarchal era, with its unity with the body, its ease with the instincts, and its openness with sexuality, was akin to Paradise—a uroboric, unconscious containment, a land of milk and honey, a virtual Garden of Eden. Those who lived in this blissful state were unaware of the narrowness of their beliefs, unaware of their one-sidedness, unaware that while honoring the body and sexuality, they were ignoring the power and necessity of the spirit and reason. The evolution of human consciousness required that the spirit's claim and position in the psyche be acknowledged. There had to be an expulsion from Paradise. There had to be a willingness to experience the neglected, unlived side. And it was the feminine, the mythical women, that led the way.

Eve's eating the apple and Athena's decision to free Orestes symbolically mark the same time period on the world stage. It was the time when the one-sidedness of the matriarchy had to end. The shadow side of the matriarchy—the reasoning intellect and the gift of the spirit—had to have its day in the sun. The biblical story of Eve eating the apple tells how the matriarchy, prompted by the life-force energy, chose to move toward consciousness. There was a price to pay for becoming conscious, and the cost was revealed at the moment when Yahweh, the patriarchal god, judged Eve and separated her from her sexuality. The Greek myths of Athena elaborate the implications of increased consciousness, showing how the matriarchy will be transformed in the process. Both myths reveal that without a knowledge of good and evil, without an awareness of paradox and a recognition that there are at least two sides to everything, human consciousness would not mature. The matriarchal era was a uroboric container that had to be broken if human consciousness was to develop. The break happened and the patriarchy emerged, suppressing what had once been supreme. Women, the body, and sexuality were all demeaned. A woman's independence and her freedom to openly express her sexuality disappeared.

A woman's body and her sexuality were no longer hers to enjoy; they were at the disposal of the patriarchy, while her worth to the culture was determined by her child-bearing capabilities or by the sexual pleasure she could give to her husband or lord and master. Women became subservient, excluded from the rings of power. No visage of woman remained in the image of the Divine.

The patriarchal era, however, is not the end point in the development of human consciousness. The patriarchy is as one-sided in its elevation of the spirit and the masculine as the matriarchy was in its honoring of the body and the feminine. With its striving for perfection, its honoring of the spirit, and its reliance on logic, the patriarchal world is now being forced to yield to a new configuration, one that will include the neglected, unlived side. Developmentally, this means that now is the time when the feminine and masculine must come into balance on the world stage. This will be seen in relationships between women and men, who will become equals, peers in a partnership. It also means that now is the time when the paradox of spirituality versus sexuality (or instinct) must be resolved.

The mythic pattern on the world stage appears once again to be on the verge of change. Old ways are being challenged. What will be birthed is not known, but there is the possibility that the pattern is shifting into something completely new.

If it is true that a relationship exists between the inner and the outer worlds, and if it is true that we are in a time of transition, then events happening now on the world stage would have to mirror changes occurring within individual psyches. Further, and of particular interest in this work, the outer changes would have to mirror the changes occurring within the psyches of father's daughters. If we are truly on the brink of change, then the art and the behavior of people on the world stage would reveal that father's daughters are reworking their myth and birthing a new pattern. It is to these contemporary developments that we now turn.

Chapter Nine

Riding the Wave of the Future

On the world stage, there are signs of change all around us. The old ways are dying. In retrospect, we have seen the mythic pattern move from matriarchy to patriarchy. Once again, the mythic pattern is in a time of transition, a time of change, giving us the opportunity for birthing something completely new. There is a feeling of chaos all around us as established patterns are disrupted by what seem to be capricious and unpredictable events. The changes appear chaotic if we are caught in the swirling mists of their unpredictability. But if we can gain a broader perspective of what is happening—and we can do this by moving into the position of the observer—we will be able to catch glimpses of the new pattern, the new mythology, emerging from the chaos. We will be able to observe only hints, but the hints will indicate the direction in which we as a culture, or as a world family, are heading.

When I began writing this book, I was caught, at first, in seeing the changing role of women as the most obvious change occurring on the world stage. The changes that are occurring for women are certainly important, but they are motivated by something deeper. As my writing and my thinking continued, I acknowledged another theme, one underlying all the changes I observed. I realized that in all the turbulence of the late twentieth century, in this creative chaos that we are living, there is no consensus as to the defining characteristics of the Divine or even to where the Divine resides. Patriarchal societies in which the Divine is seen as masculine are being shaken to their core. The exclusion of the feminine from the Godhead is being challenged, and this challenge is reflected in all the changes I observed regarding women. What are the changes in the roles of women? What are the changes for a father's daughter? And what are the changes in our conception of the Divine?

In the past few thousand years, women accepted the patriarchal view of who they were. But now women are asserting their right to freedom and autonomy, their right to choose what is to be done with their bodies, minds, and souls. They are no longer content to be defined by a man's perception of how they should be. Women are speaking up about sexual discrimination and sexual harassment. Collectively, women are no longer willing to be told by any institution of church or state what their sexuality means. Women want reproductive freedom. They want the right to choose whether or not to become pregnant and, further, they want the right to choose whether or not to terminate a pregnancy if they do become pregnant.

Women's demand for freedom and equality is being voiced in word and action around the world. Women in Japan, for example, are refusing to marry the coddled young men who expect their wives to continue where their mothers left off (see Itoi and Powell 1992). These young men believe that women exist to meet unquestioningly all their stated and unstated whims and desires. Older Japanese women who have lived their lives in subordinate roles, waiting on their husbands hand and foot, are declaring as they age that, when they die, they do not want to be buried next to their husbands. This declaration is recognized as a kind of divorce after death, and by this act these older women proclaim their disillusionment with the social system.

On the world stage, we see women emerging in new roles. We see women as warriors; indeed, it is not only in the United States that women in the military are arguing for and gaining the right to combat status. We see women no longer content with subordinate roles in organized religion. Women have gained the right to become priests in certain Christian and Buddhist groups. In other denominations, we see them pushing for equality. In the Roman Catholic church, women are pressing for ordination. In the Jewish tradition, women want rabbinical training. We see a reemergence of Gnosticism and earth-centered spirituality—both of which honor the feminine and view women and men as equals. We see women in politics, as heads of state in certain countries and governors, senators, and cabinet members in the United States. Women have entered all the professions—law, medicine, academia—not just the traditional feminine professions of nursing or teaching. What is the meaning of all the changes we are observing?

As we noted before, the drama, the myth, being played out on the outer stage reflects the drama going on within the individual psyche. The changes we observe in the roles of women are conditioned by inner transformations which are the result of interactions between these female individuals and their inner higher selves, the image of God residing within.

We often forget that the Divine did not cease interacting with human beings when the Torah, the Bible, or the Koran were written. The Divine's presence in human life did not end with the twilight of the gods. The Divine speaks today, as it always has spoken to human beings everywhere. We hear the voice in our psyches, we recognize its writings on our hearts, we see its images in our dreams and in our imaginations. There is a biblical passage (Jeremiah 31:33) that states that each person shall know the Divine personally: "This shall be the covenant that I will make with the house of Israel; After those days, saith the Lord, I will put my law in their inward parts, and write it in their hearts; and I will be their God, and they shall be my people."

The image of God within, in the Jungian perspective, is the Self, with a capital S. This is the true center of one's personality. It is the divine spark within the human being that urges one to move toward enlightenment. This center of one's being, one's inner higher Self, speaks to us in a mythic language through our art, our literature, our imaginations.

We need not refer back to previous eras to interpret what is being said to us today because our psyches are producing myths today that allow us to image our own future. In fact, as Russell Lockhart notes in *Psyche Speaks: A Jungian Approach to Self and World*, the records of mythic language from the past may be inadequate for explaining or containing what is happening in this age. He cautions that by continually looking backwards toward "Greek gods, Sumerian goddesses, Latin divinities . . . we may miss relating to the actual myth-inducing, myth-producing quality of psyche in our own time" (1982, p. 52). He continues by saying:

> The psyche has not abandoned its mythic capacity, its mythic generation, its mythic speech. Myth is not something that happened long ago and is now only repeating, remembered, re-told, or re-presented. Myth is not written once and for all. . . . Myth is speech of the psyche at any time and . . . it may not be as crucial to consciously "re-vision" or "re-voice" what has been as to become consciously involved and committed to experiencing directly the voices and visions of the spontaneous psyche in our time. (Ibid.)

81

What are the new myths that are being presented to us at this time and where are we heading—within, in our psyches, and without, in our culture? I believe that the goal for all human beings is the same, that is, that each of us is being called to be all that she or he can be. I imagine a circle, with the goal we are seeking—the fullness of being human—in the center. All individuals are standing on the perimeter of the circle, each at a particular place. Each person, if she or he is facing toward the center, can glimpse the goal at the end of the journey, yet each person follows a unique, individual path inward. It is a verification that indeed "All roads lead to Mecca." The road I have been examining is the road taken by father's daughters. And so it is fitting to ask: What are the new myths for father's daughters? What do these myths reveal about the father's daughter's journey, and where do they point for the future?

There are two stories, two modern myths, that I feel speak to the developmental process of father's daughters as they move toward the center of the circle to claim their own power and authority. These are stories that deal with father's daughters in the post-"Rumplestiltskin" era. One of the stories is Madeleine L'Engle's *A Wrinkle in Time* (1962) and the other is Mercer Mayer's *East of the Sun and West of the Moon* (1980).

What is remarkable about both tales is that, unlike fairy tales or mythic legends of the past, these tales are about ordinary people. The gods have come to earth from Mount Olympus, and the heroines of these stories are not princesses or queens, they are young women. These tales are about two modern father's daughters who find themselves separated from their fathers' love and protection. The patriarchal container is missing. Meg, the heroine in *A Wrinkle in Time,* is an awkward adolescent whose father is an absent scientist, missing in space; the marriageable maiden in *East of the Sun and West of the Moon* is the daughter of a farmer. He is unavailable to her because of his ill health. In both the L'Engle and Mayer stories, there is a new twist. The old roles of father and daughter are reversed, with the daughter assuming the heroic role—rescuing, redeeming, and healing her masculine counterparts whether he be father, brother, or lover.

Our myths are limited by our frame of reference and the ground of prior knowledge that we have attained. Space travel, for example, was always a possibility because the laws of physics and mathematics have always existed and have not changed. What precluded travel to the moon was that we as human beings did not know those laws, and so the possibility of space travel existed only in the imaginations of those who wrote science fiction. The possibility of space travel could not be actualized until the ground of human knowledge included the necessary laws of mathematics and physics, until, in other words, human beings could comprehend the probabilities.

The eternal truths of archetypes such as the father's daughter are like the laws of mathematics and physics, in that they remain constant in the psychoid reality, that is, in the depths of the unknowable mystery of the psyche. The mythic patterns and symbols related to the archetype shift and change as human beings change through enlarging their ground of self-knowledge—that is, as they become capable of comprehending a fuller picture of the truth.

Jung said, "Eternal truth needs a human language that alters with the spirit of the times. The primordial images undergo ceaseless transformation and yet remain ever the same, but only in a new form can they be understood anew" (1946, par. 396). And in *Mysterium Coniunctionis* he wrote: "All true things must change and only that which changes remains true," (1955–1956, par. 503).

New aspects of an eternal truth, such as the archetype of the father's daughter, are revealed through human imagination, through our creative potential. These new aspects of mythic patterns, which appear in artistic endeavors, are always ahead of the collective, societal consciousness. Individuals change one by one as the imagined future is incarnated in their lives. When a critical mass of individuals change, the collective consciousness changes. I believe we now are accumulating a critical mass of more conscious individuals to bring forth—to birth, if you will—something new for the collective.

In 1962, when Madeleine L'Engle wrote her book, the world was changing. The Sputnik era was underway and the United States and the Soviet Union were competing to be the first nation to put a man on the moon. Space exploration had captured the imagination of the world, affecting old beliefs, challenging old assumptions, and forcing common people and intellectuals alike to reexamine their perspectives on the world.

Many people felt threatened because their three-tiered view of the world—God above in his heaven, human beings on earth, and the devil below in hell—could no longer be sustained by the facts. The heavens were being invaded by spaceships. "God is dead," Nietzsche had announced decades before, and now those individuals with a three-tiered view of the cosmos felt the implications of his decree. Where was God if not in his heaven? Where could the Divine possibly reside? Did God exist at all? It was against this background—that is, the changing comprehension of reality—that the two myths of father's daughters I want to discuss appeared.

Young professional women have told me how influential *A Wrinkle in Time* was for them in their formative years. Meg, the protagonist in that story, became their heroine, a role model for them to follow. They, like Meg, were no longer contained within the cocoon of their father's love. Father, for them, was no longer an idealized figure. In Meg they saw an adolescent who was not precocious or beautiful. She was a young girl who didn't fit in. She had difficulty conforming to school and to collective expectations. She did not do well in areas where girls were expected to do well and excelled in areas usually reserved for boys. For example, she was gifted in mathematics. Meg misses her absent father and loyally defends his honor and his reputation even though she is confused and uncertain about what is happening.

In the story, through a series of extraordinary events, Meg finds herself in outer space—on other planets—accompanied by her younger brother and an older, gifted neighbor boy. The three of them have set out together to find Meg's father. In the course of their quest, Meg's precocious, overconfident, little brother falls victim to the intellect of a disembodied brain. It is the same intellect that has entranced and imprisoned their father. Symbolically, the story is depicting the patriarchal culture's one-sidedness in its over reliance on the intellect, on logos.

With the painful, frightening realization that she alone has the capability of rescuing her father and freeing her little brother, Meg becomes the primary force in their redemption. She learns that she must be courageous, she must become the heroine. In the course of the story, Meg learns it is love and not intellectual achievements that will provide what is needed to free her father and her little brother.

Meg is set upon her task by unseen forces, mysterious beings who call themselves Mrs. Whatsit, Mrs. Who, and Mrs. Which. These mysterious beings shape-shift and have power much greater than any human being. They are the forces of the universe that are helping Meg. In the end, however, it is not the supernatural forces that bring about the change, freeing the father and breaking the grip of the intellect. The changes occur because one individual, a frightened adolescent girl, chooses to do what she can do. In exercising her free will, just as the "Rumplestiltskin" maiden did, Meg breaks the pattern of the past and psychologically moves from being a little girl to being a heroine. The maturing feminine energy is not yet a woman, yet it is the feminine, the daughter, who redeems the father. It is not the son.

Meg rescues her father through the use of a pair of spectacles that change the wearer's perspective. The father is rescued first; the little brother is still entranced. When Meg and her father are on safe ground, she admits to him that she had wanted to remain a little girl, she had not wanted to be responsible:

> "I wanted you to do it all for me. I wanted everything to be all easy and simple. . . . So I tried to pretend that it was all your fault . . . because I was scared, and I didn't want to have to do anything myself—"
>
> "But I wanted to do it for you," Mr. Murry said.

This interaction, describing how things used to be, clearly illustrates the dynamics of a father's daughter from both the daughter's and the father's point of view. The daughter wants to be rescued, and the father wants to be the hero. Mr. Murry, Meg's father, insists that he will not let Meg go to rescue her brother. He states that he will undertake that task. This time, however, father is not to be the hero. The uncanny forces intervene, reminding him that this is Meg's task—one that she has chosen to do—and so Meg's father withdraws his objections. Meg remembers that her mother would want her to do this. She remembers that her mother was always encouraging her, pushing her out into the world. With the remembrance of that inner encouragement, Meg undertakes the rescue of her brother and succeeds. She breaks his enchantment by loving him. As the tale ends, everyone returns safely to earth.

In *East of the Sun and West of the Moon*, the story is not science fiction for children but a modern fairy tale. Mayer takes the traditional tale of the frog prince and reworks the elements, going beyond the "And they lived happily ever after" ending. In the original fairy tale, the story ends after the princess breaks the spell by which the prince had been transformed into a frog.

The original tale begins with a princess wiling away her time playing with a golden ball in the garden. The ball rolls into a pond, falling beyond her reach. A frog retrieves the golden ball for her after he obtains a promise from the princess to grant him three wishes.

The princess returns home with her ball, thinking no more about her promise. But the frog does not forget. The frog follows her home.

Begrudgingly, the princess grants him two wishes: one, she allows him to visit at the castle and, two, she allows him to eat off gold plates. When the frog states his third wish, that the princess share her bed with him and become his bride, the princess refuses. The frog speaks to the king, informing the king of the promise the princess had made. The king insists the princess keep her word and grant the frog's third wish. In her bedroom, the enraged princess smashes the frog against the wall. Her anger and her actions free the prince from his enchantment. This old fairy tale reveals how women could survive in a repressive, patriarchal culture without developing a victim mentality. The anger of the princess was an appropriate defense against depression. It was also a defense against passive-aggressive compliance with oppressive societal values.

In the reworked tale, a few of the basic ingredients have been altered. Not a princess but the daughter of a farmer is the heroine who grants three wishes to a frog. The maiden is not wiling away her time playing in a garden, she is working. She is on a mission charged by her mother to obtain water from a particular spring to cure her ailing father. Another critical factor that is different is that it is a silver cup that is dropped in the well, not a golden ball.

The maiden returns home, and her father is healed by the water she brings. Other than the mentioned differences, the story is similar to the original tale up until the point when the enchanted frog appears at the maiden's house and asks for her hand in marriage. As in the original tale, the maiden smashes the frog against the wall. A handsome youth emerges, but here the story changes. Because the maiden chose not to marry him, the youth is carried away by trolls to a land east of the sun and west of the moon where he is to be married to a troll princess. This modern fairy tale is stating that the old ways, the anger, is not enough. It is hinting that there must be a relationship, a conscious choosing by both parties.

The maiden, regretting her angry actions, begins a journey to rescue her beloved. She travels to the four corners of the earth, asking for help. She speaks to the fiery salamander, to Father Forest, to the Great Fish of the Sea, and to the North Wind. Each gives her advice and gifts she can use to effect the rescue of her beloved—a tinder box, a bow and arrow, and a fish-scale mirror. When the North Wind deposits her at the troll castle, the maiden uses her wits and the tools she has been given to rescue the young man and free others enchanted in the land east of the sun and west of the moon.

With the tinder box, the maiden starts a fire that melts the icy casket of the young man; with the bow and arrow she shoots the troll princess in the heart; and with the fish-scale mirror she reflects back to the remaining trolls their hideousness, turning them to stone. With that, their power of enchantment is gone. The young maiden and the youth are married, and they form a new land. The young maiden and the youth are equals. Their marriage is a relationship between peers.

The ending of the tale states that arriving at that destination either within oneself or in relationship with another is not an easy task. We are told that forevermore, people will know the directions to that new land are difficult to follow and there is no guarantee of ever reaching it. However, if and when one does arrive, there will be the warm reception of a homecoming.

In both of these tales, it is the daughters' actions—their becoming heroines—that is crucial. Both of these young women exercised their free will and chose to heal and redeem the masculine. The mothers of these daughters were unable to rescue or cure their spouses. They were caught in old, traditional roles. However, in both tales, the mothers were potent influences in their daughter's lives because they were women who honored the feminine. These mothers gave their daughters encouragement for being female and pushed them into action.

Meg's mother continued her research in a room off of the kitchen. She fostered her daughter's independence as she herself struggled to combine the roles of mother and scientist. In the modern fairy tale, the mother gives her daughter a silver cup—a symbol of the feminine containing energy—as she charges her with the task of finding the water that will cure her father. Neither maiden was told by her mother that she had to yield or conform to society's expectations for women.

Both *A Wrinkle in Time* and *East of the Sun and West of the Moon* depict a transitional time in the lives of father's daughters. They indicate that on the world stage, the pattern of a father's daughter is shifting. The patriarchal structure can no longer contain this feminine energy. The daughter is becoming a heroine. She is putting away childish things and learning to accept her own unique power. She is no longer relying on daddy to protect her. She sees the limitations of her father and recognizes the shortcomings of the patriarchy. However, she is not out to destroy the patriarchy, but to heal it. She knows that although the patriarchal culture has achieved many things, there is a power within the feminine energies that must be tapped and utilized. There must be a new relationship, a true relationship, between the masculine and the feminine.

The heroines in these tales are adolescent girls, not yet mature women. On the world stage, these stories tell of a new reality, a recognition that the patriarchal culture is not well and that it is young feminine energy that will redeem the father, brother, and lover. What will the myth or the culture be like when the feminine is mature and the masculine is healthy? That is the myth of the future. The two stories we examined tell of the growing pains of father's daughters as they move from dependence into heroism. What, we may then ask, will father's daughters look like when they become women of power?

Chapter Ten

The Magic of Beginnings

As the story is told, Amaterasu omi-kami, the powerful Japanese sun goddess, was given three gifts: a sword, a jewel, and a mirror. All three symbolized different aspects of her imperial power. The tale is recounted by Alvin Toffler in his book *Powershift* (1990, p. 13), in which he examines the changing base of power in our current world. The sword and the jewel symbolize might and money, respectively, and represent the ways in which power traditionally has been gained and maintained. With the sword, for example, one gains physical mastery, resulting in independence for oneself and domination over others. Amaterasu omi-kami, not surprisingly, is especially revered by the Samurai warriors and students of the martial arts in Japan. With the jewel, or money, one is able to wield economic power, again gaining independence for oneself and control over others. The third gift, the mirror, allows Amaterasu omi-kami to see herself and, through reflection, to gain self-awareness. This is the most powerful of her three gifts, we are told, because the mirror symbolizes her divinity. Until the goddess sees herself, until she reflects and learns who she truly is, she is unaware that she is divine.

The myth of Amaterasu omi-kami's three gifts tells us that the image of the Divine lies within. It lies unacknowledged, however, until through reflection, the image is seen. For women living in the patriarchal era in which the Divine was conceptualized as exclusively male, seeing the image of the Divine within themselves was a difficult task. Today, with the feminine dimension of the divine once again being acknowledged (Engelsman 1994), the task of looking for the divine image within is less daunting, not only for father's daughters but for all women. Younger women will definitely have an easier time recognizing and accepting the divine image of the goddess within themselves than their mothers did.

In the two stories discussed in the previous chapter, *A Wrinkle in Time* and *East of the Sun and West of the Moon*, the differences between the mothers and their daughters were clearly delineated. The mothers of the young heroines were unable to break completely with the patterning of the past. They were not able to free themselves from the roles prescribed by the culture. Yet they had made a significant shift from their predecessors in how they regarded their feminine core. Where their mothers and grandmothers had denied, even renounced, the power of the feminine, these mothers honored it and passed on to their daughters pride in being born female.

In *East of the Sun and West of the Moon* pride in the feminine is symbolized by the silver cup the maiden receives from her mother as she sets out on her task to obtain the water that will heal her father. The maiden sets out on her journey, her first warrior's task, not with a spear or golden armor, but with a silver cup, symbolizing the containing, holding, relationship aspect of the feminine. The silver cup marks a significant shift in the mythic pattern on the world stage. In the myth of Athena, for example, the goddess is born wearing golden armor which she sheds, but she does not replace it with anything made of silver. Gold, as we have noted, symbolizes the masculine, silver symbolizes the feminine. On the world stage, at the time of Athena's birth, the power of the feminine had to remain hidden. In *East of the Sun and West of the Moon*, the mother had taken over the leadership of the family because her husband had fallen ill. She was doing all she could to heal her spouse and reestablish their relationship. However, the healing of her husband's sickness was beyond her capabilities. It was a task she handed to her daughter.

In the other story we examined, *A Wrinkle in Time*, the mother is an educated woman. She has been trained as a theoretical physicist. She does not work on her own, however, but in partnership with her husband. The task of being a parent, of nurturing their four children, also falls to her. She is both mother and scientist, and although motherhood restricts her freedom, it does not stop her professional pursuits. She works in her laboratory, adjacent to the kitchen, combining motherhood with scientific research, cooking stew on a Bunsen burner in her lab. This mother encourages her daughter, Meg, to be all that she can be, to move out into the world and experience all that life has to offer although she herself stays at home while her husband is lost in space. Meg's mother is incapable of bringing her husband to earth.

The mothers in both of those stories encouraged and pushed their daughters to break free of societal constraints. The young heroines in those two tales typify contemporary father's daughters who, in breaking free of the old patterns, suddenly find themselves in radically changed environments. These modern women look around and realize their land is a wasteland. They realize that their expectation of living in a green valley where they will be cared for and protected is an illusion. No one is going to take care of them. They discover, sometimes painfully, that they will have to take care of themselves.

The picture of society given to us by the two tales, in my opinion, accurately reflects what father's daughters, and for that matter, most young adults, are experiencing today. They are realizing that our society is barren. In one of the tales, it is the king's wars that have depleted the country's resources. In the other tale, it is the nation's drive to control space that has resulted in the imprisonment of the loving father. In both stories, it is conflict and competition, war and the desire to dominate, that leaves the land and the family bereft.

We are in a wasteland. The old tales of the Grail legend with Parsifal traveling to the wounded king accurately describe the barrenness of our patriarchal culture. Those tales, related from a male perspective, tell of a man's need to reconnect with the feminine, to honor women. But the truth is that the change needed in our society will not be accomplished by men. The new society will be birthed by women, and it will be preceded by a new myth.

In *A Wrinkle in Time* and *East of the Sun and West of the Moon*, father's daughters were depicted as teenagers, symbolizing that the emerging feminine is not yet mature. In the new myth, the teenagers will be transformed into women of power. The new myth, now being birthed, is rooted in the recognition that the feminine and all that is female can no longer be subsumed within the masculine ethos. The new myth, where the feminine is equal to the masculine, will be embodied by women who are peers to their male partners, women who are not looking to men, whether father or husband, to take care of them. Father's daughters and, for that matter, all women must grow into autonomous human beings who, through their own independence and free will, choose to dance with, unite with, and marry another independent person.

The work on one's self is the critical issue. Father's daughters must look into their mirrors and heed the image of the Divine within. The dwarf must become the hero — an inner shift that will be reflected in the outer world when women become equal partners with men. But this is only an intermediate step. The final step occurs when father's daughters become women of power and move into the magical position of being co-creators of their worlds. This can only happen when the feminine is as highly regarded within the personality as the masculine and a union, a marriage, of these equal forces occurs.

Jung described the inner marriage of the feminine and the masculine as the goal of the individuation process. There is, however, a shortcoming in Jung's conceptualization and in his use of alchemy as a symbolic metaphor for achieving an inner *coniunctio*.

Although he was a visionary pioneer, Jung was limited by being a product of the Victorian era. His progressive vision of a masculine/feminine balance was limited by the ground of knowledge upon which he stood and the *Zeitgeist*, the spirit of the times, in which he lived. Although he envisioned abstractly a psychological marriage of masculine and feminine energies, with both energies being equally valued, concretely, he did not see men and women as equals. In regard to their creative energies, he saw women as supporting the creative spirit of men. Women were to be the inspiration of men, with a woman's animus fertilizing the man's anima (1928, par. 336). Many authors have wondered where Jung saw a woman's creativity residing (Singer 1976, p. 47; Douglas 1993).

Holding the explicit position of psychological equality between the masculine and the feminine energies while paradoxically maintaining the tacit assumption of inequality between men and women, Jung drew upon the symbolism of alchemy to amplify the process of the inner conjunction. The metaphor was useful to him in illuminating not only the inner marriage, the *coniunctio* within the personality, but also in describing the transformation that occurs in the analytic process of transference and countertransference, whereby both analyst and analysand are in the bath.

The feminine and masculine union in alchemy results in a marriage of Sol and Luna — the sun and the moon. The sun is the illuminator in our solar system, the moon, rotating around the earth, is a celestial body reflecting the sun's light. When the alchemical marriage is completed, a two-headed androgyne or hermaphroditic figure results. However, this marriage of sun and moon is not a marriage of equals. The moon in a certain sense is the handmaiden to the sun. It is seen only when it catches and reflects the rays of the sun, otherwise it remains in darkness, unseen. There is a similarity between the moon reflecting the sun's glory and the father's daughter who finds her purpose in life by shining before the eyes of her father.

It may be that the alchemical metaphor expressed the very best of what was possible in the Victorian era between the feminine and the masculine or between a woman and a man: namely, that a balance of Sol and Luna would occur, that a woman would find her glory in reflecting the glory of a man. Such a marriage suggests that a woman could not attain the balance of masculine and feminine within and without, and neither could a man, because the marriage was not a marriage of equals. There are other shortcomings in the alchemical marriage of Sol and Luna. Their heavenly union is an ungrounded marriage of celestial spheres. It is a marriage of energies in the spirit world and therefore lacks substance.

Further, regardless of the progressive states of blackness or redness described in the alchemical process and regardless of the tempering by salt or sulfur, the aim of alchemy, stated over and over again, is to free the spirit locked in matter, in earth, and to return the spirit to the light. This suggests that light and spirit are the desired goals and that matter and the body are corporeal prisons. The alchemical marriage of Sol and Luna is not a union of equals; it is an ungrounded subsuming of the feminine by the solar masculine energies. The alchemical marriage of Sol and Luna, however, accurately portrays the union of a father's daughter with her masculine partner, as well as the inner marriage for any individual where the feminine is subordinate to the masculine.

Jung's vision of an inner marriage of the feminine and masculine went beyond the prevailing attitudes of his culture. But the truth is, he was not completely free of the spirit of his age, and his use of alchemical symbolism to amplify his ideas reveals the limitations imposed upon him by the culture in which he lived. The alchemical metaphor is an old myth and it is inadequate today for explaining or amplifying the inner marriage in which a woman honors her feminine side as well as her masculine side. The alchemical metaphor is another instance of old skins being unable to stretch and hold the new wine.

If the image of the *coniunctio* is to be relevant for our current age—that is, if the symbol is to be a guiding image for contemporary women and men—the inner marriage must be a marriage between equals, a partnership, a joining together of the light and the dark, of the spirit and the body. The guiding image cannot be a marriage of the sun and the moon—because they are not equals—but it could be a marriage between the sun and the earth. This union, the marriage of sun and earth, would symbolize the dance between spirit and substance, where spirit becomes substance and substance returns to spirit. The masculine sun brings illumination and imagination which are given form, incarnated in the body, and actualized by the feminine earth. And, as in all cases where two seemingly opposite energies are united, the transcendent third will be birthed. This means that within the human personality, the divine image will be realized when the inner marriage between the feminine and masculine as equals is accomplished.

What does this mean for a father's daughter or, for that matter, anyone who has been serving the father gods? It means that the father's daughters, and others, will begin emanating their own power. They will no longer be striving to reflect their father's glory at the expense of their own truth. Symbolically Logos—the spirit and the mind—will be married to Eros—the sensual, instinctive, body knowing. These contemporary father's daughters will reclaim their right to hold their own values and find their own truths. They will refuse to accept male or masculine judgments on how they should be, knowing these judgments derive from a strictly male perspective (Gilligan 1982). We can ask what would the *coniunctio*, the marriage of the feminine and masculine energies within a woman's personality, look like when the feminine is held in as high regard as the masculine?

We know from our cursory examination of the mythic patterns on the world stage that a fundamental difference between the matriarchal and patriarchal cultures lay in their treatment of sexuality and the body. The matriarchy celebrated sexuality and the instincts; the patriarchy devalued sexuality and the body while valuing the spirit and the mind. As father's daughters step forward into a new myth, a return to goddess worship—that is, to an honoring of the body and sexuality without an accompanying honoring of the spirit—would be regressive, a step backward in time. Too much is known today about Logos and the importance of the spirit to exclude either from the divine face. In the new myth, father's daughters will have to reclaim their instincts and sexuality while maintaining their intellectual and spiritual achievements. This is the marriage, the blending, that is required if the mythic pattern on the world stage is to move forward in terms of human evolutionary consciousness.

The future calls for a new image, a new divinity, perhaps a partnership between goddess and god. In this partnership, there will have to be a union of sexuality and spirit, a blending of the instinctual body and the reflective mind. This blending is an acceptance and honoring of both the powerful divine forces operating in human lives—feminine and masculine.

Although at first glance sexuality and spirituality appear to be diametrically opposed, and indeed they have been opposed in the matriarchal and the patriarchal eras, they are related, as Jung has noted; indeed, they are two sides of the same coin. Jung wrote, in explaining his position:

> Sexuality is not mere instinctuality; it is an indisputably creative power that is not only the basic cause of our individual lives, but a very serious factor in our psychic life as well . . . We could call sexuality the spokes[person] . . . of the instincts, which is why from a spiritual standpoint sex is the chief antagonist, not because sexual indulgence is in itself more immoral than excessive eating and drinking, avarice, tyranny, and other extravagances, but because the spirit senses in sexuality the counterpart equal and indeed akin to itself. For just as the spirit would press sexuality, like every other instinct, into its service, so sexuality has an ancient claim upon the spirit, which it once—in procreation, pregnancy, birth, and childhood—contained within itself, and whose passion the spirit can never dispense with in its creations. Where would the spirit be if it had no peer among the instincts to oppose it? It would be nothing but an empty form. (1948, par. 107)

As father's daughters step forward to reclaim their sexuality for themselves, they may, as Eric Neumann noted (1969, p. 90), have an encounter with the devil. The devil, in the Judeo-Christian-Islamic tradition, embodies all that is excluded from the light, incorporating all that the patriarchy decrees to be immoral, improper, unethical, or unclean. Paradoxically, however, the devil is called Lucifer, whose name means "bringer of the light." Encountering Lucifer indicates symbolically that one's beliefs and values must be reexamined. Father's daughters must determine if the beliefs and values they hold are valid for themselves, and they must discern whence those beliefs and values came.

The passage in the Old Testament book of Jeremiah (31:31–35) concerning a new covenant between God and his people states that the new law will not be found within the temples or taught by the priests or the rabbis. It is a law written on one's heart. It is an inner truth that has been there all through our lives, but that has remained unseen because we did not look within to find it. For a woman of power, it is a truth that cannot be avoided.

Now is time for father's daughters and all individuals to find their truth. It is time for them to look into their mirrors, as Amaterasu omi-kami did, to see who they truly are and to recognize the image of the goddess and the god within.

In the Jungian framework, as human beings move toward increased consciousness, each person moves at her or his own pace. The process is a dance between the ego and one's higher Self. The higher Self encompasses all that is possible and stretches the imagination of the ego with its communications of symbol and myth. The ego determines which possibilities to incarnate into life and does the necessary work to make the image a reality. In looking into our mirrors, as Amaterasu omi-kami did, we will encounter the image of the goddess and the god within. Actualizing the divine image is an awesome responsibility. It means we must become magicians, creators of our own worlds. Just as Black Elk, in his vision, saw himself as the center pole of the universe, each of us, likewise, must see herself as the center pole of her own unique universe. We are to be magicians, and as magicians we imagine what is possible and then actualize it in our lives. We are no longer limited by one persona.

Becoming a magician, the individual accepts the gifts and the short-comings in her personality. She stays open to learning from her personal shadow as well as the collective shadow while maintaining an open heart-to-heart connection with the Self. She chooses how she wants to be seen, varying the hat she wears according to the circumstances and her desires.

The resolution for a father's daughter, as she becomes a magician, is not to dominate men. It is to begin a cooperative dance with men as an equal. It is time for her to put away childish things, to stop being a handmaiden to the lord, and to anoint herself as a woman of power. It is time for her to become her own champion and to take responsibility for her choices. It is a time for her to become autonomous in the full sense of the word. She is to be self-naming, that is, she is to name herself. No longer will she be content with others telling her who she is and how she should behave.

Reclaiming her sexuality is one of the first tasks that an autonomous father's daughter will accomplish. This does not mean that she will necessarily end old relationships, but it does mean that she will no longer engage in sexual relationships out of a sense of duty or a need to

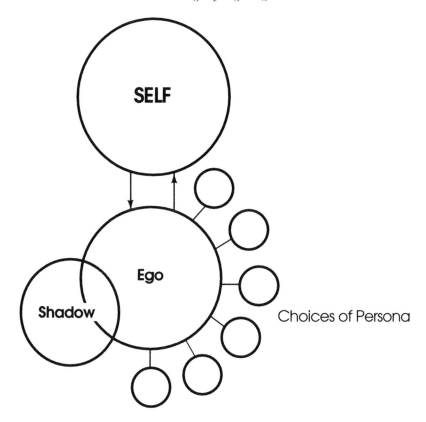

Fig. 12. The options of a magician: the hats one can wear

please someone else. By receiving the pleasure of her own sexuality, she will be reclaiming her fire, the energy and passion that provide the fuel required to make changes.

In alchemy, the retort was fired, heated, to cause the transformation. In *East of the Sun and West of the Moon*, the first place the maiden travels is through the ice caverns to reach the alchemical fire. Without the fire she would not have had the energy needed to complete her tasks. Women's fire was contained under the patriarchy, and whatever was expressed came out as anger, rage, or hysteria. A woman had little energy she could use for herself.

As the father's daughter assumes her own authority and becomes autonomous, she becomes more willing to speak her truth and champion her own values. While appreciating others who affirm her stance, she is willing to stand alone if that is what her truth requires. Becoming a magician, the father's daughter will no longer be dependent on her father for approval and security. She has matured, she is no longer a teenager, and she has removed the restrictive glasses, rose-colored or not, that caused her to view reality as she thought a father's daughter should view it. She now sees reality as it truly is, and in exercising her freedom and her free will she moves and changes according to reality. She dances with the universe, with the forces greater than she, and accepts synchronistic occurrences as a matter of fact. As Carol Pearson notes in *The Hero Within:*

> While Warriors learn the rules of cause and effect, Magicians learn those of magic. Magic works acausally. . . . The Magician understands grace—not as an unusual occurrence, but simply as one kind of energy available to us. . . . Magicians strive . . . to live in harmony with the supernatural and the natural worlds, and doing so requires wholeness and balance within. . . . While Magicians have a kind of humility in understanding that we are only a small part of the great ongoing activity of creation, claiming co-creation with God is an act of great self-assertion. (pp. 118–120)

Self-assertion requires that an individual be willing to stand up and be counted and, when asked, to speak her truth. This is not always easy. In the summer of 1991, I had an experience of having to stand and be responsible for my truth, my inner knowing, despite what I feared might be collective disapproval. I had planned to be in northern Michigan and, unexpectedly, I was asked to create and conduct a ceremony for a group of people in that area while I would be there. The group that requested my participation was a diverse conglomeration of individuals who originally had come together in 1987 to mark the Harmonic Convergence. They had continued to gather together each subsequent year during the summer. Their ceremonies in the past had been joined by some of the Native American people from the area. In fact, on each previous occasion, a sacred-pipe carrier had participated and conducted a pipe ceremony as part of the observance. I was not certain what I would do and, because the primary reason I was in northern Michigan had nothing to do with this gathering, I had not given much thought to their request.

As the time approached, it felt right for me to do a pipe ceremony, one that I had been taught was appropriate for special group gatherings. But it was not without misgivings that this decision was reached. I was experiencing a great deal of conflict. I knew that in most of the tribes of the Plains Indians, including the tribes in Michigan, women were not pipe-carriers. Although most of these Indian tribes could have and did have women elders, they were primarily patriarchal, with the roles of men and women clearly defined. Here I was, a middle-aged white woman without a drop of Indian blood, stating that I was a pipe-carrier and planning to do a pipe ceremony in public.

There were about fifty of us who gathered that afternoon, young and old, male and female. We formed a circle, sitting on the grass under shade trees beside a brook. When I looked up, I saw, sitting directly opposite me, a full-blood Indian male. My heart jumped. I took a deep breath, I knew who I was. I was not pretending to be anything other than who I was. As we began the ceremony, I told my story to the group—how I had come to the teachings, who my teacher was, and who his teachers were. I acknowledged that the tradition I was learning was but one of the ways, not the only way to relate to the Great Spirit. Other traditions, I stated, were just as valid as the tradition I studied.

We created a medicine wheel and I explained about the smudge as I lit it and spread the smoke with a fan. I told how the smudge would purify, bless, and balance with beauty, and I explained about the elements in the four directions. I taught how I had been taught to pray with the pipe and explained how they could pray with the pipe when it was passed around the circle. I answered questions and then, as I filled the pipe and spoke my prayers, the group was silent and attentive. After I had smoked, it was my turn to be silent and attentive, watching while the pipe was passed from one to the other clockwise around the circle, nearer and nearer to the Indian sitting opposite me. Now, it was his turn. He smoked the pipe, passed it to the person on his left, then rose and walked toward me. My heart skipped a beat. I wondered what was going to happen. I had stepped into my power and now I wondered what his reaction was going to be.

He stood in front of me, his hand extended, offering me a gift. I received it, held it to my heart, and nodded to him, wordlessly thanking him for his gift. I could see that it was a package of tobacco that he had been using. He had wrapped it with cedar and sage and tied it with a blue ribbon. I looked at him and he took my right hand and held it between his two hands. There were tears in his eyes and tears were now falling down my cheeks. I knew that tobacco, sage, and cedar are sacred and they are gifts one gives to a teacher or to someone one wants to honor. This six-foot-tall Native American was acknowledging me, a white grandmother, as someone he wanted to honor. He walked back to his place on the circle. I continued to sit, my heart full, tears falling, marveling at what had transpired. The universe had cooperated in a way that I never could have imagined.

I later learned from the man who had organized the gathering that these Indian people have a legend about the evolution of the world and the people in it. The legend teaches that there is a developmental series of worlds and as one world ends another begins. Harmony and completeness, the legend states, will come with the fifth world when human beings everywhere see themselves as members of one family. It is also told that in the fourth world, the white man will dominate the red man. The people, the Indians, will know that the fourth world is ending and the fifth world is beginning when white people accept and honor the Indians' sacred ways.

Standing up for one's truth and accepting the responsibility for one's decisions is the process of actualizing what has been written on one's heart and what one sees in the mirror. This process is like a double helix, spinning inward and spinning outward at the same time. It is a dancing with the universe and a dancing with oneself, each movement feeding the other, reaching new levels of Self-awareness in both realms. If there is a symbol for this unending process, it could be an infinity sign made with a rebus loop, with one's will located at the crossover point in the figure eight.

To make this symbol, imagine a piece of paper that is black on one side and white on the other. If you cut a long narrow strip of paper and fasten the ends together so that white meets white and black meets black, you would have a loop, or circle, where one color is on the inside and the other on the outside. You could draw a continuous line either on the outside of the loop or on the inside, but not on both without lifting your pencil. The circle can be twisted in half so that it forms a figure eight, but it would still have one color on the outside and the other on the inside. Now, when you were making the loop for the first time, if one of the ends had been turned over before it was attached so that black met white and then the ends were fastened together, you would have created a rebus loop. With a rebus loop, a continuous pencil line can be drawn, starting anywhere, that will mark both sides of the loop. Now if you make the rebus loop into a figure eight, you have an infinity movement which spins in both directions, a loop where there is no beginning and no ending.

Becoming a magician, with the outer world mirroring the inner

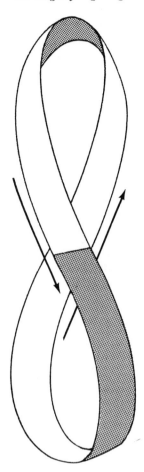

Fig. 13. The rebus loop

world and the inner world feeding the outer world, the father's daughter replaces her inner dwarf with a partner, not just a servant like the queen's messenger in "Rumplestiltskin." Her inner elevation of the masculine in a more helpful form is compensated in consciousness by the daughter moving into her womanly stature. No longer does she demean the feminine vis-a-vis the masculine in the outer world as she had in the daughter-father dyad. It is now adult woman to adult man in both worlds. In the outer world, this would mean that the father's daughter who yielded unquestioningly to male authority figures now becomes the peer, the equal of these men. Now she questions their judgments, statements, and requests. She ponders and then decides whether to accede or disagree. She has married her feminine and masculine energies both within and without, and she is free to pick from a variety of personae, donning whatever mask is appropriate for the moment. She is the magician.

The changes the father's daughter makes will be mirrored on the world stage. The divine image held by the collective will shift from being limited to a patriarchal deity to a new image that includes both feminine and masculine aspects. In relationships between men and women, there will also be a shift. No longer male-dominated, relationships will become partnerships between men and women, a collaboration of equals. Women and men, both, will become magicians, co-creators of their world. It will be a time of fulfillment when each person who moves to become a magician will be an incarnation of love or, as some Indians say, a cell of the Great Spirit's body, touching oneself, life, and others with beauty.

For those who are magicians and those who are striving to become magicians embodying love, I offer this paraphrase of a Navajo prayer:

> May you walk with Beauty
> With Beauty before you
> With Beauty behind you
> With Beauty all around you.

And may you remember trailing clouds of glory at your birth.

Epilogue

In 1982, Murray Stein suggested that I consider writing a book on the positive father complex. I had just completed my training to be a Jungian analyst and had written my diploma thesis on Athena. He told me about two theses written by women who had already completed their Jungian training. One, by Florence Wiedemann, was on Brunnhilde, the other, by Ruth Goodwin, was on Helen of Troy. He suggested that we three women might collaborate in writing a book. I followed up on his suggestion, exploring with my two colleagues the possibility of our working together. All of us thought it was a good idea; however, at the time none of us had the energy to take the initiative in organizing such an endeavor.

The idea lay fallow for several years, gestating, not ready to be born. I presented bits and pieces of this material at different times to various groups and was met with mixed reviews. In some instances, the presentation was a painful stillbirth. At other times, there was some vitality but the material had not coalesced into its proper form; it was still premature. In 1991, almost ten years after Murray's initial suggestion, I began to work in earnest. This time, however, the work refused to take the form I originally had envisioned. *Her Father's Daughter* was stubborn and determined to have a life of its own. No wonder the previous presentations were incomplete. I had been way off track.

Hundreds of pages that I had written were discarded into the wastepaper basket. I consoled myself with the thought that the hours I had spent producing those writings were not wasted but necessary. The material I had been studying, my own life experiences, and the work I was doing with clients all had to be placed into the alchemical pot. The time I had spent laboring over the manuscript in the previous years was a time of stirring the chaotic, alchemical stew. Examining the lives of mythical father's daughters was a necessary ingredient, but those mythic lives were not enough. What I discovered was that more had to go into the pot than I had originally imagined. Stirring the alchemical pot was a time of transformation. Finally there was a cohesion, a coalescing, and the parts united in a new way into a work I had not envisioned.

When I presented this material in 1992 and 1993, much of it in the form it is presented in here, the reception was positive, even enthusiastic. I knew the time for birthing was near.

This work is my offering to forward the dream of a society where women and men work in partnership, honoring each other without exploitation. It is a society in which nothing is done to harm the children, whether it is human children, the children of Grandmother Earth, or one's own inner child.

The gift that returns to me with this book is the enrichment that will come to me when some of you decide to utilize the methods discussed here to further your own individuation process. It is a fact that when one person changes, becoming more conscious, more aware, every human being benefits. It may be that you will embrace a new myth for yourselves, perhaps even the myth of becoming a magician.

I am indebted to my friends and family who read the manuscript and pointed out areas that needed clarification or expansion. Thank you, Brenda Donahue. Thank you, Frances Ritzinger. I am also indebted to four individuals who first introduced me to Jungian psychology through their connections to the Educational Center in St. Louis and later their connections to Centerpoint. Two of these individuals — Perry Porter and Elsom Eldridge — are deceased, so my thanks to them is posthumously expressed. To the two others — Hazel Porter and Chandler "Chink" Brown — I extend my thanks for the many mirrors they held for me, mirrors in which I could see my own reflection. And, of course, nothing would be complete if I did not express my gratitude to my husband, Bob, and to my children and grandchildren for the joy they bring into my life and the teachings they continually give me.

Mary Loomis
Grosse Pointe, Michigan
October 1993

Bibliography

Bolen, J. S. 1984. *Goddesses in Everywoman*. San Francisco: Harper and Row.

Downing, C. 1981. *The Goddess: Mythological Images of the Feminine*. New York: Crossroad.

Douglas, C. 1993. *Translate This Darkness: The Life of Christiana Morgan, the Veiled Woman in Jung's Circle*. New York: Simon and Schuster.

Edinger, E. 1972. *Ego and Archetype*. New York: Putnam.

Eisler, R. 1986. *The Chalice and the Blade*. San Francisco: Harper and Row.

Eliot, C., ed. 1937. *Folklore and Fable: Aesop, Grimm and Andersen*. New York: P. F. Collier and Son, Harvard Classics.

Engelsman, J. C. 1994. *The Feminine Dimension of the Divine*, rev. ed. Wilmette, Ill.: Chiron Publications.

Fraser, J. G. 1922. *The Golden Bough*. New York: Macmillan.

Freitas, M. 1981. Electra: The redemption of the feminine. Lecture given at the C. G. Jung Institute, Evanston, Ill.

Gilligan, C. 1982. *In a Different Voice*. Cambridge, Mass.: Harvard University Press.

Graves, R. 1948. *The White Goddess*. New York: Farrar, Straus and Giroux.

_____. 1977. *The Greek Myths*. 2 vols. New York: Penguin Books.

Grene, D., and Lattimore, R. 1959. *Aeschylus*. Chicago: University of Chicago Press.

Hillman, J. 1980. *Facing the Gods*. Dallas: Spring Publications.

Itoi, K., and Powell, B. 1992. Take a hike, Hiroshi. *Newsweek*, August 10, pp. 38–39.

Jung, C. G. 1928. The relations between the ego and the unconscious. In *CW* 7:123–304. Princeton, N.J.: Princeton University Press, 1953.

_____. 1946. The psychology of the transference. In *CW* 16:163–326. Princeton, N.J.: Princeton University Press, 1954.

_____. 1948. On psychic energy. In *CW* 8:3–66. Princeton, N.J.: Princeton University Press, 1960.

_____. 1951. *Aion. CW*, vol. 9ii. Princeton, N.J.: Princeton University Press, 1959.

_____. 1954. Psychological aspects of the mother archetype. In *CW* 9i:75–110. Princeton, N.J.: Princeton University Press, 1959.

_____. 1955–1956. *Mysterium Coniunctionis. CW*, vol. 14. Princeton, N.J.: Princeton University Press, 1963.

_____. 1958. The transcendent function. In *CW* 8:67–91. Princeton, N.J.: Princeton University Press, 1960.

Karen, R. 1992. Shame. *The Atlantic* 269(2):40–70.

Kerenyi, K. 1978. *Athene: Virgin and Mother in Greek Religion*, M. Stein, trans. Zurich: Spring Publications.

L'Engle, M. 1976. *A Wrinkle in Time*. New York: Farrar, Straus and Giroux, Inc.

Loomis, M. 1982. A plea for wisdom. Unpublished thesis. Evanston, Ill.: C. G. Jung Institute of Chicago.

_____. 1990. *Dancing the Wheel of Psychological Types*. Wilmette, Ill.: Chiron Publications.

Lockhart, R. 1982. *Psyche Speaks: A Jungian Approach to Self and World*. Wilmette, Ill.: Chiron Publications.

Mayer, M. 1980. *East of the Sun and West of the Moon*. New York: Four Winds Press.

Meador, B. 1987. Uncursing the dark. Lecture presented to the American Jung Societies, Chicago, Ill.

_____. 1992. *Uncursing the Dark: Treasures from the Underworld*. Wilmette, Ill.: Chiron Publications.

McGrew, L. 1989. Shame and the paralysis of feminine initiative: An analysis of Athene-Persephone women. Unpublished thesis. Evanston, Ill.: C. G. Jung Institute of Chicago.

Neumann, E. 1974. *The Great Mother*. Princeton, N.J.: Princeton University Press.

Owens, L., ed. 1981. *The Complete Brothers Grimm Fairy Tales*. New York: Avenel Books.

Pagels, E. 1982. Whatever happened to God, the Mother? Lecture presented to the C. G. Jung Institute, San Francisco.

Pagels, E. 1988. *Adam, Eve, the Serpent*. New York: Random House.

Pearson, C. 1987. *The Hero Within*. San Francisco: Harper and Row (Harper-Collins Publishers Inc.)

Shuttle, P., and Redgrove, P. 1978. *The Wise Wound*. New York: Macmillan.

Singer, J. 1976. *Androgyny: Toward a New Theory of Sexuality*. New York: Doubleday.

Stevens, C. 1985. The feminine self: Concept, image and clinical significance. Unpublished thesis. Chicago: The Chicago Society of Jungian Analysts.

Sun Bear and Wind, W. 1990. *Black Dawn/Bright Day*. Spokane, Wash.: Bear Tribe Publishing.

Toffler, Alvin. 1990. *Powershift*. New York: Bantam Books.

Wiedemann, F. 1979. Brunnhilde—A representative of "The Eternal Feminine." Unpublished thesis. The Interregional Society of Jungian Analysts.

Young-Eisendrath, P., and Wiedemann, F. 1987. *Female Authority: Empowering Women Through Psychotherapy*. New York: Guilford Press.

Index

DATE DUE

GAYLORD			PRINTED IN U.S.A.